Lois Levine's

VEGETABLE
FAVORITES

Lois Levine's

VEGETABLE FAVORITES

Illustrations by Hugh McMahon

Cover photograph by Victor Scocozza

GOLDEN PRESS • NEW YORK
WESTERN PUBLISHING COMPANY, INC.
RACINE, WISCONSIN

INTRODUCTION

I'm a dyed-in-the-wool vegetable fan. And, fortunately, so are all the members of my family. Consequently, I've spent years collecting and creating vegetable recipes — always looking for recipes that are unusual or sure to please or easy but exciting or even difficult but worth the trouble. As a result, I've discovered — or, rather, confirmed — that vegetables, without question, are among the most versatile of foods.

Naturally, the healthiest and best-tasting vegetables come fresh from the garden. Many can be grown easily in your own backyard, even in a tiny patch. The tomato is a good do-it-yourself vegetable that seems to flourish anywhere, and the plants produce prolifically until the end of the season. Zucchini is another example. In fact, our zucchini grows in such abundance that we are often inundated from the produce of just one plant. Even city dwellers with sunny windowsills or rooftop space can grow a variety of vegetables in pots or boxes.

Come harvest time — each vegetable in its season — chances are you will have more "just-picked" vegetables than your family can eat. Canning is complicated and time consuming, but if you have the patience for it, be sure to get expert advice on exact procedures. For me, freezing is far easier. Most fresh vegetables require just a quick blanching before they can be frozen. Also, many vegetable dishes can be partially or fully prepared and then frozen. And throughout this book I have indicated which dishes freeze particularly well.

If your own vegetable garden is not a possibility, look around for a farmers' market. Native produce in season is still the best to buy — best quality, often best price. For a great part of the time, however, most of us must rely on the local supermarket, where fresh produce can usually be found year round. Lettuce, for example, always seems to be available in at least one of its many varieties. I prefer the tender leaves of Boston or romaine from my own garden, but a bit of fresh iceberg from California can be pretty tempting in the middle of winter.

Of course, canned and frozen vegetables are always available. Don't turn up your nose at them. Consider the convenience of a can of tomatoes when you're struck with a last-minute midwinter urge for tomato sauce after your own freezer has given up its last batch. Or think of the times when you're grateful for those tiny frozen peas that don't have to be shelled. While these canned or frozen counterparts may not taste quite as good as fresh, there are many times — even for the most discriminating cook — when convenience has to be the overriding factor.

Although vegetables traditionally have been considered main-course accompaniments, I'd like to introduce you to some delicious exceptions: change-of-pace hors d'oeuvres (Asparagus Roll-Ups, Petite Potato Pancakes); earthy, fragrant soups of eggplant or mushroom; refreshing salads (Peas with Dill, Curried Artichoke); vegetable breads; even vegetable desserts — Pumpkin Crunch Pie, and a chocolate cake made with . . . sauerkraut!

Of course, vegetables can also stand on their own as main dishes for lunch and dinner. I often serve Stuffed Eggplant, Spinach Sauce with Fettucini or Golden Harvest Bean Pot in place of meat. I think well-balanced vegetable meals are healthy, and they break the monotony of the meat/starch/vegetable menu routine to which so many of us fall prey. Moreover — and this is no small consideration in these inflationary times — they are economical, especially when the vegetables are home grown.

You will note that I have not tried to make this book botanically complete. Many vegetables are omitted — most of them uncommon ones, others that simply are not among my favorites. (You'll quickly discover which vegetables I like best, since the number of recipes is heavily weighted in their favor.) For convenience, the book is arranged alphabetically by vegetable. I've indicated how many servings each recipe will allow for and, when applicable, which recipes can be made in advance and either refrigerated or frozen. In some instances, the servings may seem generous. Admittedly, I find it somewhat difficult to judge. In my family we don't have many vegetable leftovers, but we do have lots of second helpings.

Here's hoping that you, too, will be serving a lot of vegetable second helpings — and enjoying every bite!

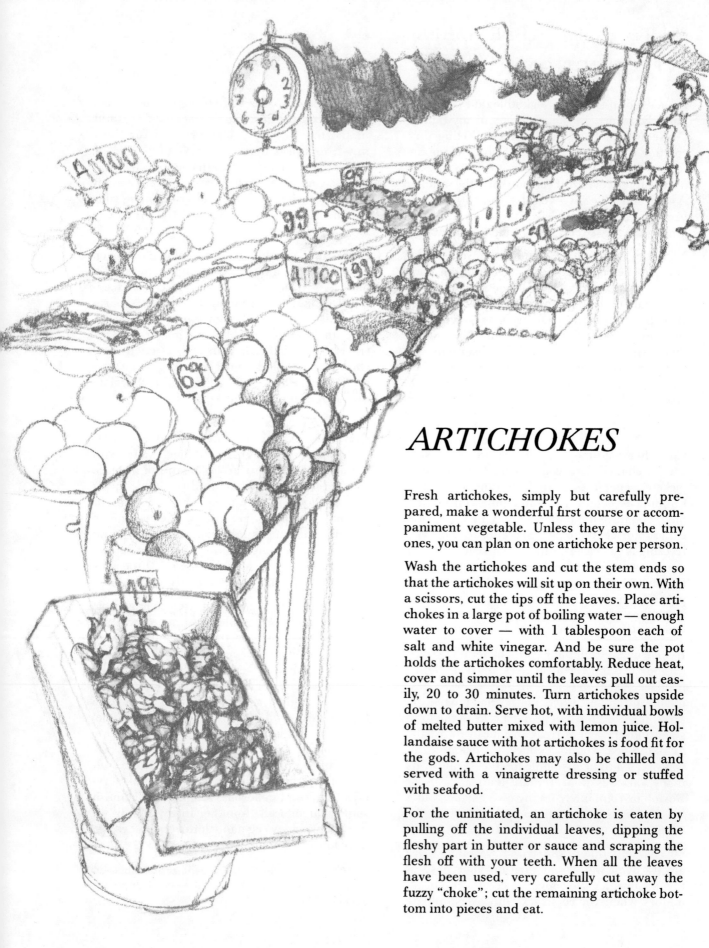

ARTICHOKES

Fresh artichokes, simply but carefully prepared, make a wonderful first course or accompaniment vegetable. Unless they are the tiny ones, you can plan on one artichoke per person.

Wash the artichokes and cut the stem ends so that the artichokes will sit up on their own. With a scissors, cut the tips off the leaves. Place artichokes in a large pot of boiling water — enough water to cover — with 1 tablespoon each of salt and white vinegar. And be sure the pot holds the artichokes comfortably. Reduce heat, cover and simmer until the leaves pull out easily, 20 to 30 minutes. Turn artichokes upside down to drain. Serve hot, with individual bowls of melted butter mixed with lemon juice. Hollandaise sauce with hot artichokes is food fit for the gods. Artichokes may also be chilled and served with a vinaigrette dressing or stuffed with seafood.

For the uninitiated, an artichoke is eaten by pulling off the individual leaves, dipping the fleshy part in butter or sauce and scraping the flesh off with your teeth. When all the leaves have been used, very carefully cut away the fuzzy "choke"; cut the remaining artichoke bottom into pieces and eat.

ARTICHOKE APPETIZERS

2 jars (6 ounces each) marinated artichoke
  hearts
1 medium onion, finely chopped
1 clove garlic, minced
4 eggs, lightly beaten
¼ cup dry bread crumbs
¼ teaspoon oregano
⅛ teaspoon hot pepper sauce
2 cups shredded Cheddar cheese
2 tablespoons minced parsley
  Salt and pepper

Drain marinade from artichoke hearts, reserving the marinade from one of the jars. Chop artichoke hearts into small pieces and reserve.

In a small skillet, heat reserved marinade and sauté onion and garlic 5 minutes. Combine remaining ingredients with the reserved artichokes and the onion mixture. Turn into a greased 13 x 9 x 2-inch baking dish and bake at 325° for 30 minutes. Cool in pan. Cut into squares.(*)

About 3 dozen.

(*) May be refrigerated up to 24 hours or frozen. To serve, cover with foil and bake at 325° until heated through, about 20 minutes.

CURRIED ARTICHOKE SALAD

½ cup mayonnaise
1 tablespoon capers
1 clove garlic, crushed
1 teaspoon curry powder
¼ teaspoon Worcestershire sauce
  Dash hot pepper sauce
½ teaspoon dry mustard
1 jar (6 ounces) marinated artichoke hearts,
  drained
8 cups salad greens (spinach, romaine, endive)

To prepare dressing, blend mayonnaise, capers, garlic, curry powder, Worcestershire sauce, hot pepper sauce and mustard. Chill at least 1 hour.

When ready to serve, cut artichoke hearts into small pieces and toss with salad greens. Pour dressing over all and toss.

Serves 4.

BAKED ARTICHOKE HEARTS

1 can (15 ounces) artichoke hearts, drained
3 tablespoons olive oil
½ cup dry bread crumbs
½ teaspoon salt
¼ teaspoon pepper
¼ teaspoon oregano
¼ teaspoon basil
1 clove garlic, crushed
2 tablespoons grated Parmesan cheese

Cut artichoke hearts in half and arrange cut side up in an 8 x 8 x 2-inch baking pan. Sprinkle with 1 tablespoon of the oil. Combine bread crumbs, seasonings, garlic and cheese and sprinkle over hearts. Moisten with remaining oil. Bake at 325° for 10 minutes and then broil until golden brown, 3 to 5 minutes.(*)

Serves 4.

(*)May be refrigerated up to 24 hours. To serve, cover with foil and bake at 325° until heated through, about 20 minutes.

ARTICHOKE PIE

  Pastry for 10-inch pie shell and top crust
2 packages (8 ounces each) frozen artichoke
  hearts
3 tablespoons olive oil
2 onions, finely chopped
1½ cups freshly grated Parmesan cheese
1 cup ricotta cheese
  Dash freshly ground pepper
8 eggs

Prepare pastry. Line pie plate for shell; reserve top crust.

Cook artichoke hearts as directed on package and drain. Cut into bite-size pieces. In a skillet, heat olive oil and sauté onions until translucent. Combine onions and artichokes with cheeses, pepper and 4 of the eggs, lightly beaten. Mix well and spoon into unbaked pie shell. Make 4 depressions in mixture and break 1 egg into each depression. Cover with reserved pastry; seal edges. Make steam holes in pastry.(*)

Bake at 450° for 10 minutes. Reduce heat to 400° and bake until pastry is light brown, 30 minutes longer. Allow to stand 10 minutes.

Serves 6 as a main dish.

(*)May be prepared in advance to this point. Refrigerate up to 24 hours or freeze. To serve, bring to room temperature and bake as directed above.

ASPARAGUS

Be sure to select asparagus stalks that are of uniform thickness, with tightly closed buds. Two pounds of fresh asparagus will serve four.

Wash carefully, snap off tough ends and pare away any large scales on the stalks. The French steam asparagus by standing it upright, in several inches of water, in the bottom half of a double boiler with the top half inverted to cover the asparagus tips. I find that cooking it lying down in a small amount of salted water just long enough to make the asparagus tender, is quite right for me. I cannot be exact about cooking time since this varies with the thickness of the stalks. As a rule, allow 5 to 10 minutes and test with a fork.

Serve with melted butter and lemon juice or, if you feel like splurging, with hollandaise sauce. Cold asparagus with a vinaigrette dressing makes a lovely salad.

BROILED ASPARAGUS ROLL-UPS

20 medium spears fresh asparagus
6 to 8 ounces sharp Cheddar cheese
1 pound loaf sliced sandwich bread
½ cup soft butter
1 tablespoon chopped parsley
½ teaspoon dill weed
3 tablespoons sliced green onions
¼ cup butter, melted

Wash asparagus and discard tough ends. Cover and simmer until tender, 5 to 10 minutes; drain. Cut cheese into 40 slivers. Trim crusts from bread and roll slices with rolling pin.

Combine ½ cup soft butter with parsley, dill and green onions and spread evenly on one side of each bread slice. Top with 1 asparagus spear and 2 cheese slivers. Roll up and secure with toothpicks.(*) Arrange on a foil-covered baking sheet and brush with melted butter. Broil 5 inches from heat until golden, 3 to 5 minutes.

20 appetizers.

(*)May be prepared in advance to this point. Refrigerate up to 24 hours or freeze. To serve, bring to room temperature and broil as directed above.

ASPARAGUS SOUP

1½ pounds fresh asparagus
¼ cup butter
½ onion, minced
4 cups chicken broth
⅛ teaspoon ground nutmeg
Salt and pepper to taste

Wash asparagus and discard tough ends. In a large skillet, melt butter and sauté onion 3 minutes. Add asparagus and cook 1 minute longer. Add broth and seasonings. Cover and simmer until asparagus is tender, 5 to 10 minutes. Pour into blender and blend until smooth.(*) Serve hot or chilled.

Serves 6.

(*)May be refrigerated up to 48 hours or frozen.

ASPARAGUS AND AVOCADO SALAD

    2 pounds fresh asparagus
    2 tablespoons red wine vinegar
    6 tablespoons olive oil
    1 teaspoon Dijon-type mustard
    1 teaspoon lemon juice
    1 teaspoon salt
    ¼ teaspoon pepper
    6 to 8 radishes
    1 avocado, peeled and cut into ½-inch cubes

Wash asparagus and discard tough ends. Cut off tips and set aside. Cut stalks into 1-inch pieces. Drop stalks in boiling salted water, cover and boil 2 minutes. Add tips and boil 2 minutes longer; drain and chill.

To prepare dressing, combine vinegar, oil, mustard, lemon juice, salt and pepper. Pour over avocado. Trim radishes and slice very thin. Add to avocado. Add asparagus and toss lightly; chill (may be refrigerated up to 24 hours).

Serves 6.

ASPARAGUS QUICHE

    1½ pounds fresh asparagus or 2 packages
          (10 ounces each) frozen asparagus
          spears, thawed
        Unbaked 9-inch pie shell
     8 slices bacon
    ½ pound Swiss cheese, grated
     4 eggs
    1½ cups light cream or half-and-half
    ⅛ teaspoon nutmeg
        Salt and pepper to taste

Heat oven to 400°. Wash asparagus, cover and simmer until tender, 5 to 10 minutes; drain and reserve. Bake pie shell about 10 minutes — it should only be partially baked.

Cook bacon until crisp; crumble. Sprinkle on bottom of pie shell. Gently mix asparagus and cheese. Place on pie shell. Beat remaining ingredients and pour over asparagus.(*) Reduce heat to 375° and bake 40 minutes or until knife inserted in center comes out clean.

Serves 6 as a main dish.

(*)May be prepared in advanced to this point. Refrigerate up to 24 hours. To serve, bring to room temperature and bake as directed above.

CHINESE BEEF WITH ASPARAGUS

    1 pound flank steak
    1 tablespoon soy sauce
    1 tablespoon water
    1 tablespoon honey
    1 clove garlic, crushed
    ¼ teaspoon ground ginger
    1 teaspoon salt
    4 tablespoons dry sherry
    8 spears fresh asparagus
    1 tablespoon cornstarch
      Rind from ½ orange, slivered
    4 cloves garlic, minced
   10 slices gingerroot
    ½ cup broken walnuts
    3 tablespoons peanut oil

Cut the meat into 2¼x½-inch slices. Combine soy sauce, water, honey, crushed garlic clove, ground ginger, salt and sherry. Pour over meat and let stand at least 30 minutes. Drain meat, reserving marinade.

Cut asparagus into 2-inch lengths and cook in boiling water 2 minutes; drain. Combine 1½ teaspoons of the cornstarch with 2 tablespoons of the reserved marinade and stir into meat. Mix remaining cornstarch with reserved marinade; reserve.

Combine orange rind, minced garlic, gingerroot and walnuts; reserve.

In a wok or large skillet, heat oil and stir-fry meat until it changes color. Add the reserved orange rind mixture and asparagus to wok and toss. Stir in reserved cornstarch-marinade mixture and stir-fry until meat is glazed. Serve immediately.

Serves 4 as a main dish.

AVOCADOS

Although avocados seem exotic to many people, they are in fact both nourishing and practical. They can be used as an appetizer, soup, salad, vegetable dish or a colorful garnish. Half of an avocado, an average serving, contains only 138 calories, but is loaded with vitamins A, C and E and contains no cholesterol. In addition, and most important, avocados are simply delicious. An extra bonus is the fact that the pit can be rooted and grown into a beautiful plant in your home.

GUACAMOLE DIP

- 3 ripe avocados, peeled and pitted
- 1 large tomato, peeled and chopped
- 4 green onions, chopped
- 3 tablespoons lemon juice
- 1 teaspoon Worcestershire sauce
- 3 drops hot pepper sauce
- ½ teaspoon salt
- ⅛ teaspoon pepper

Mash avocados with a silver fork (to prevent them from turning dark). Mix with remaining ingredients, cover and chill (may be refrigerated up to 24 hours). Serve with corn chips as dippers.

About 3 cups.

AVOCADO DIP

- 1 large ripe avocado, peeled and pitted
- 1 tablespoon lemon juice
- 1 tablespoon vinegar
- 1½ teaspoons salt
- ¾ teaspoon sugar
- 1 tablespoon grated onion
- 1 clove garlic, mashed
- 1 cup sour cream
- 2 tablespoons grated Parmesan cheese

Mash avocado with a silver fork (to prevent it from turning dark). Mix in remaining ingredients and refrigerate at least 2 hours to blend flavors (may be refrigerated up to 72 hours). Serve with tortilla chips as dippers.

About 3 cups.

COLD AVOCADO SOUP

- 2 cans (10 ounces each) cream of potato soup
- 2½ cups milk
- 2 ripe avocados, peeled and pitted
- ⅛ teaspoon hot pepper sauce
- ⅛ teaspoon white pepper
- ⅛ teaspoon chili powder
- ½ teaspoon salt
- 6 tablespoons sour cream

Heat soup and milk, stirring until smooth. Mash avocados with a silver fork (to prevent them from turning dark) and stir into soup. Add seasonings and heat through. Cool slightly, then puree in a blender or food processor. Chill at least 2 hours (may be refrigerated up to 24 hours). Serve cold, garnished with dollops of sour cream.

Serves 6.

AZTEC ASPIC

2 cans (12 ounces each) vegetable juice
    cocktail
3 envelopes unflavored gelatin
1 can (10¾ ounces) condensed tomato soup
½ cup canned whole kernel corn, drained
2 tablespoons chopped green pepper
½ cup cold water
1½ cups mashed avocado (about 2 avocados)
¼ cup mayonnaise
½ teaspoon grated lemon rind
1 tablespoon lemon juice
1 tablespoon grated onion
½ teaspoon salt
1 teaspoon prepared horseradish
½ cup heavy cream, whipped
    Salad greens

In a small saucepan, combine 1 cup of the vegetable juice cocktail with 2 envelopes of the gelatin. Heat very slowly, stirring until gelatin is completely dissolved.

In a large bowl, combine tomato soup, remaining vegetable juice and the gelatin mixture; chill slightly. Stir in corn and green pepper. Turn into a 2-quart mold and chill until set.

In a small saucepan, combine water and remaining gelatin. Heat slowly, stirring until gelatin is completely dissolved. Combine gelatin with avocado, mayonnaise, lemon rind and juice, onion, salt and horseradish. Chill until mixture mounds slightly, then fold in whipped cream. Spread avocado mixture over set tomato layer. Chill at least 4 hours, until firm (may be refrigerated up to 48 hours). Unmold on greens.

Serves 6.

AVOCADO MOUSSE

1½ tablespoons unflavored gelatin
⅓ cup water
2 ripe avocados, peeled and pitted
¼ cup lemon juice
1 teaspoon salt
¼ teaspoon garlic salt
4 drops hot pepper sauce
1 cup heavy cream, whipped
    Lettuce leaves
    Lemon wedges

Sprinkle gelatin on water to soften, then set over boiling water. Stir to dissolve.

Mash avocados with a silver fork (to prevent them from turning dark) and blend pulp with lemon juice, salt, garlic salt and hot pepper sauce. Stir in dissolved gelatin and fold in whipped cream. Turn into a lightly oiled 1-quart soufflé dish; cover and chill 1 hour or until completely set (may be refrigerated up to 24 hours). When ready to serve, unmold on lettuce leaves and garnish with lemon wedges.

Serves 6 to 8.

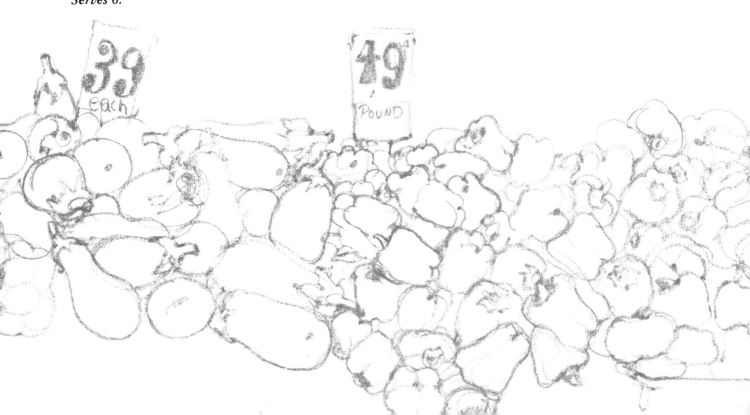

BEANS

If you aren't lucky enough to grow your own supply of garden-fresh green beans, try to buy them young and crisp. You can tell if they're fresh by the ease with which you can snap them in half.

Wash the beans and snap them in half. Remove any strings. Drop the beans in boiling salted water (just enough to cover) and cook, covered, until barely tender, about 20 minutes. Small whole beans will be tender in about the same amount of time. If the beans are cut French style, 10 minutes will be ample. Drain and serve with butter, salt and pepper. One pound of fresh green beans will serve four.

For variety, season them with tarragon, celery seed, rosemary or dill. A touch of garlic and a drop of olive oil, instead of butter, will give the beans an Italian flavor. Although it has really been done to death by new brides and old caterers, beans may be dressed up with slivered almonds or sliced sautéed mushrooms. Pearl onions may be used, too. Frankly, I think fresh beans are much too good for all that jazz. Save the fussing for the off-season, when you have to resort to frozen beans — they need all the help they can get.

Lima beans can be used fresh, frozen or dried. Whatever variety your recipe calls for, limas should not be overcooked (fresh, about 10 minutes, depending on the size; frozen and dried, according to package directions). Dried beans require soaking, often overnight. Some, of course, come already prepared in cans, waiting only for your added touches. Don't overlook their many possibilities.

SICILIAN GREEN BEANS

  2 pounds fresh green beans
  ¼ cup olive oil
  1 bunch green onions with tops, chopped
  ½ cup chopped parsley
  1 clove garlic, minced
      Salt and pepper to taste
      Pinch oregano

Wash beans and trim ends. Parboil 5 minutes. In a large skillet, heat oil and add beans. Sprinkle with remaining ingredients. Sauté on all sides. Reduce heat and add 3 tablespoons water; cover and steam 20 minutes.

Serves 6.

SPICY GREEN BEANS

  2 tablespoons peanut oil
  1 teaspoon minced gingerroot
  ½ teaspoon minced garlic
  ½ pound fresh green beans, trimmed and slivered
  1 teaspoon sugar
  2 tablespoons dry sherry
  ½ teaspoon salt
  2 teaspoons chili paste with garlic (buy in Chinese grocery)
  2 tablespoons soy sauce
  ½ teaspoon cornstarch
  1 tablespoon water
  1 teaspoon sesame oil

In a wok or skillet, heat peanut oil and stir-fry gingerroot and garlic 30 seconds. Add beans and stir-fry 2 to 3 minutes. Mix in sugar, sherry, salt, chili paste and soy sauce. Stir-fry 1 to 2 minutes longer. Combine cornstarch and water and add to pan. Cook until mixture thickens. Remove from heat and stir in sesame oil. Let cool, then chill at least 2 hours (may be refrigerated up to 24 hours). This may also be served hot, but it is basically a cold dish.

Serves 4.

SWEET-AND-SOUR BEAN SALAD

    1 can (16 ounces) cut green beans
    ½ cup white vinegar
    ½ cup sugar
    1 teaspoon celery seed
    ¼ teaspoon dry mustard
    1 can (8 ounces) wax beans, drained
    1 medium onion, sliced into rings
    2 tablespoons chopped green pepper
    2 tablespoons chopped pimiento
      Boston lettuce cups

Drain liquid from green beans and reserve. In a saucepan, combine reserved liquid with vinegar, sugar, celery seed and mustard; bring to a boil.

In a large bowl, combine green beans, wax beans, onion, green pepper and pimiento. Pour boiling vinegar mixture over beans; cover and chill (may be refrigerated up to 24 hours). Drain and serve in lettuce cups.

Serves 6.

SWISS GREEN BEAN CASSEROLE

    1 package (9 ounces) frozen French-style
        green beans
    1 cup sour cream
    2 tablespoons grated onion
    ½ teaspoon salt
    ¼ teaspoon white pepper
      Dash cayenne pepper
    ¾ cup grated Swiss cheese

Cook beans according to package directions until crisp-tender; drain. Mix sour cream and onion. Season with salt, white pepper and cayenne. Combine sour cream mixture with beans.

In a buttered 1-quart casserole, layer beans and grated cheese, making 2 layers of each.(*) Cover and bake at 350° for 30 minutes. Uncover and bake 15 minutes longer to brown top.

Serves 4.

(*)May be prepared in advance to this point. Refrigerate up to 24 hours. To serve, bring to room temperature and bake as directed above.

LIMA BEAN AND PEAR CASSEROLE

    ½ pound dried lima beans
    ½ cup light brown sugar
    ¼ cup butter
    1 can (8¾ ounces) sliced pears
      Salt to taste

Soak dried lima beans in water for several hours or overnight. Cover the pot and boil beans in the soaking water until tender, about 30 minutes.

Drain beans, reserving the liquid, and place beans in a greased 1-quart casserole. Cover with half the sugar and dot with half the butter. Drain pears, reserving juice, and place on top of beans. Cover with remaining brown sugar and butter. Pour reserved pear juice over all and bake, uncovered, at 350° until pears are brown, about 1 hour. If casserole looks dry, baste with reserved bean liquid. Be sure to taste and correct with salt as needed.(*)

Serves 4 to 6.

(*)May be refrigerated up to 48 hours. To serve, bring to room temperature and reheat.

LIMA BEAN, CORN AND CARROT CASSEROLE

    2 tablespoons butter
    2 tablespoons flour
    1 cup milk
    1 teaspoon dill weed
    ½ teaspoon salt
      Freshly ground pepper
    2 cups cooked lima beans (fresh, frozen
        or dried)
    1 cup cooked corn (fresh, frozen or canned)
    1 cup coarsely grated raw carrots
    ¼ cup grated Parmesan cheese

In a large skillet, melt butter and stir in flour. Remove from heat and slowly add milk. Return to heat and cook, stirring, until thick and bubbly. Add dill, salt and pepper. Combine vegetables and sauce and pour into a greased 2-quart casserole. Sprinkle with cheese(*) and bake at 350° for 35 to 45 minutes, until bubbly and cheese is brown.

Serves 6.

(*)May be refrigerated up to 24 hours. To serve, bring to room temperature and bake as directed above.

EDITH'S CHILI CON CARNE

    2 tablespoons vegetable oil
    1 large onion, chopped
    1 green pepper, chopped
1½ pounds ground beef
    2 cans (16 ounces each) stewed tomatoes
    1 can (8 ounces) tomato sauce
    2 cans (16 ounces each) red kidney beans,
      drained
    1 tablespoon chili powder

In a large skillet, heat oil and brown onion and green pepper. Crumble in beef and brown. Stir in tomatoes, tomato sauce, kidney beans and chili powder. Cover and simmer 1 to 2 hours. Make at least a day ahead since chili improves with reheating.(*)

If desired, serve on cooked spaghetti, 1 pound for this amount of chili.

Serves 6 as a main dish.

(*)May be refrigerated up to 48 hours or frozen. To serve, bring to room temperature, reheat and serve as directed above.

GOLDEN HARVEST BEAN POT

    1 can (28 ounces) Boston-style baked beans
    1 tablespoon Dijon-type mustard
    ⅓ cup maple syrup
    ¼ cup chopped onion
    ⅓ cup buttermilk
    ¼ teaspoon baking soda
    1 egg
1¾ cups corn muffin mix

Combine beans, mustard, maple syrup and onion in a buttered deep 2-quart casserole. Stir buttermilk and baking soda together; add egg and combine with corn muffin mix. Stir until moist but still lumpy. Spread over beans.(*) Bake, uncovered, at 375° for 25 minutes.

Serves 8.

(*)May be prepared in advance to this point. Refrigerate up to 48 hours. To serve, bring to room temperature and bake as directed above.

BEAN SPROUTS

If you don't have a Chinese grocery handy, bean sprouts are easily grown at home. Most health food stores (and they seem to be popping up everywhere) can get you started with a crop of sprouts.

CHINESE VEGETABLE SOUP

3 cups chicken broth
½ cup fresh bean sprouts, washed and drained
  (see Note below)
1 cake bean curd (buy in Chinese grocery), cubed
½ cup diced bamboo shoots
½ cup sliced fresh mushrooms
1 tablespoon soy sauce
  Dash hot pepper sauce

Bring broth to a boil. Add remaining ingredients, cover and simmer 3 minutes.(*)

Serves 4.

(*)May be refrigerated up to 72 hours or frozen. To serve, reheat.

BEAN SPROUT SALAD

1 pound fresh bean sprouts (see Note)
2 tablespoons dark soy sauce
1 tablespoon cider vinegar
1 teaspoon sesame oil
2 tablespoons toasted sesame seeds

Place bean sprouts in a bowl of cold water and remove green seed pods as they float to the surface. Drain sprouts, then drop into boiling water and simmer 1 minute; drain thoroughly. Place sprouts in a bowl with soy sauce, vinegar and sesame oil; chill (may be refrigerated up to 24 hours). When ready to serve, top with toasted sesame seeds.

Serves 4.

Note: If fresh bean sprouts are not available, you may substitute the canned variety, but they should be placed in a strainer and washed well with cold water.

BEETS

QUICKLY DELICIOUS BORSCHT

  1 can (10½ ounces) beef bouillon
     Juice of 1 lemon
     Grated rind of ½ lemon
  1 can (16 ounces) beets, undrained
     Sour cream

Put all ingredients except sour cream in a blender or food processor and blend until smooth; chill (may be refrigerated up to 48 hours). Serve topped with dollops of sour cream.

Serves 4.

BEET SALAD MOLD

  1 jar (32 ounces) borscht, with beets
  2 packages (6 ounces each) lemon gelatin
  1 can (16 ounces) shoestring beets
 ½ cup sour cream
  1 teaspoon lemon juice
     Lettuce leaves

Bring borscht to a boil and dissolve gelatin in it. Drain shoestring beets and add liquid to gelatin mixture; reserve beets. Refrigerate gelatin mixture until partially set, about 20 minutes. Mix in reserved beets, the sour cream and lemon juice. Pour into a greased 2-quart mold and refrigerate until set, at least 4 hours (may be refrigerated up to 48 hours). Unmold on lettuce leaves.

Serves 8 to 10.

PICKLED BEETS

  6 beets
  1 small onion, thinly sliced and separated into rings
  2 bay leaves
  1 clove garlic, thinly sliced
 ⅓ teaspoon marjoram
 ¼ teaspoon nutmeg
  1 teaspoon salt
 ½ teaspoon pepper
 ½ cup olive oil
 ½ cup red wine vinegar
 ½ cup red wine

Boil or steam beets until tender, about 30 minutes; cool. Peel beets and slice thinly. In a shallow bowl, place a layer of beet slices and top with a layer of onion rings. Sprinkle with broken pieces of bay leaf, a few slices of garlic, a dash marjoram, nutmeg, salt and pepper. Repeat layers until beets and onion have all been used. Combine oil, vinegar and wine and pour over all. Refrigerate at least 1 hour. Drain off most of the liquid (may be refrigerated up to 72 hours). Serve very cold.

Serves 6.

BEET GREENS WITH BABY BEETS

  2 bunches beet greens, with baby beets attached
  2 tablespoons butter
     Juice of ½ lemon

Wash greens and beets very carefully. Place in a small amount of salted water, cover and cook until tender, about 6 minutes. Drain and serve with butter and lemon juice.

Serves 4.

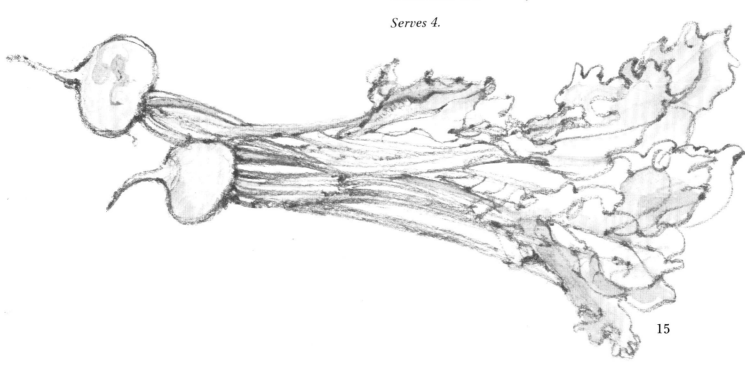

AUNT EVIE'S BROCCOLI SAUCE

    2 tablespoons butter
    2 tablespoons flour
   ¾ cup vegetable cooking water
  1½ teaspoons prepared white horseradish
    1 cup sour cream
   ½ teaspoon thyme
       Salt and pepper to taste

In a skillet, melt butter and stir in flour. Gradually add vegetable water, stirring until smooth. Add remaining ingredients and stir until heated through.

This is also marvelous over asparagus, green beans or even cauliflower. When serving over cauliflower, use red horseradish for a bit of color.

About 2 cups.

CREAM OF BROCCOLI SOUP

    2 packages (10 ounces each)
         frozen chopped broccoli
    3 tablespoons butter
   ¼ cup minced onion
    3 tablespoons flour
    3 cups skim milk
    2 teaspoons salt
       Dash pepper
    2 teaspoons grated lemon rind
    2 tablespoons lemon juice

Cook broccoli according to package directions; drain well and reserve 1 cup liquid.

In a large skillet, melt butter and sauté onion 5 minutes. Stir in flour and gradually add milk. Stir until mixture comes to a boil. Add chopped broccoli and reserved broccoli liquid; heat through. Season with salt, pepper, lemon rind and juice. (*)

Serves 6.

(*)May be refrigerated up to 48 hours or frozen. To serve, reheat.

BROCCOLI

For some strange reason, California broccoli is still the best kind to buy in my home state of Connecticut, but if you should buy native broccoli, be sure to soak it in plenty of warm salted water 10 to 20 minutes before using. If there are any worms, they'll float to the surface. Drain the broccoli well and remove any large leaves and the tough outer part of the stalks.

Place the broccoli in a saucepan in about 1 inch of boiling salted water; cover and simmer 10 to 12 minutes, until just tender. Drain and serve with butter and lemon juice, or with cider vinegar, salt and freshly ground pepper. Buttered crumbs are nice on top. A large bunch of broccoli will serve four.

Sauces for broccoli are numerous. There's hollandaise, of course, but cheese sauce, sour cream sauce and herbed mayonnaise are all good. Aunt Evie's Broccoli Sauce (right) is a fine topping, too. Chilled broccoli with a vinaigrette sauce and a garnish of pimiento is lovely in the summer.

BROCCOLI HOLIDAZE

  2 pounds fresh broccoli or 2 packages
        (10 ounces each) frozen broccoli spears
 ½ teaspoon salt
  1 can (10½ ounces) cream of chicken soup
 ½ cup mayonnaise
 ¼ teaspoon curry powder
     Juice of 1 lemon
 ½ cup dry bread crumbs
  2 tablespoons butter, melted

Wash fresh broccoli and separate flowerets. Cut stems into ½-inch slices and cook in boiling salted water 5 minutes. Add flowerets, cover and cook until crisp-tender, 8 to 10 minutes longer. (Cook frozen broccoli according to package directions.) Drain broccoli and place in a 2-quart casserole; sprinkle with lemon juice.

Combine soup, mayonnaise and curry powder and pour over broccoli. Top with bread crumbs and drizzle with melted butter.(*) Bake, uncovered, at 350° for about 20 minutes, until bubbly.

Serves 8.

(*)May be prepared in advance to this point. Refrigerate up to 24 hours. To serve, bring to room temperature and bake as directed above.

BROCCOLI BISQUE

1½ pounds fresh broccoli
3½ cups chicken broth
  1 medium onion, quartered
  2 tablespoons butter
  1 teaspoon salt
  2 teaspoons curry powder
     Dash pepper
  2 tablespoons lime juice
  8 lemon slices
 ½ cup sour cream
  1 tablespoon chopped chives

Wash and trim broccoli. In a large saucepan, combine broccoli, broth, onion, butter, salt, curry powder and pepper. Bring to a boil; reduce heat, cover and simmer 10 minutes.

Place half the broccoli mixture in a blender or food processor and blend until smooth; repeat. Stir lime juice into blended broccoli mixture. Cover and chill at least 4 hours. (*)

To serve, pour into individual bowls and garnish with a lemon slice and a dollop of sour cream. Sprinkle with chives.

Serves 8.

(*)May be refrigerated up to 72 hours or frozen.

CHINESE-STYLE BROCCOLI

  1 pound fresh broccoli
  2 tablespoons peanut oil
  1 teaspoon salt
 ½ teaspoon sugar
 ½ cup chicken broth

Wash broccoli and cut flowerets from stems. Trim off tough parts of stems and cut stems into 1-inch circles. Parboil stems and flowerets 5 minutes; drain.

In a wok or large skillet, heat oil and stir-fry broccoli just to coat with oil. Add salt and sugar; mix well. Pour in chicken broth, cover and cook 5 minutes longer. Uncover and cook over high heat until liquid is absorbed.

Serves 4.

BROCCOLI SALAD

1½ pounds fresh broccoli
 ¼ cup white vinegar
 ¼ cup sesame oil
  4 teaspoons sugar
  1 teaspoon salt

Wash and trim broccoli; discard leaves and cut into bite-size pieces. Cover and cook broccoli in a large pot of boiling salted water 3 minutes. Drain and rinse with cold water; drain again. Chill until ready to serve.

To prepare the dressing, combine vinegar, oil, sugar and salt; chill. When ready to serve, toss broccoli with dressing.

Serves 6.

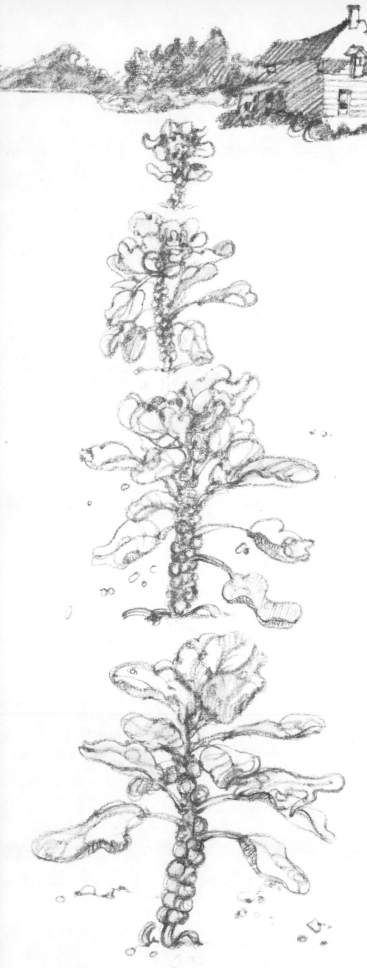

BRUSSELS SPROUTS

BRUSSELS SPROUTS WITH MUSTARD SAUCE

    2 pounds fresh Brussels sprouts
    3 tablespoons butter
    ¼ cup chopped onion
    3 tablespoons flour
    1 cup chicken broth
    1½ teaspoons dry mustard
    2 tablespoons tarragon vinegar

Place sprouts in a small amount of boiling salted water, reduce heat, cover and simmer until just tender, 6 to 8 minutes; drain.

In a separate pan, melt butter and sauté onion until limp. Stir in flour and add remaining ingredients. Cook, stirring, until smooth and thickened. Serve over sprouts.

Serves 6.

NUTTY BRUSSELS SPROUTS

    1 package (10 ounces) frozen Brussels sprouts
    2 tablespoons butter
    ¼ pound fresh mushrooms, sliced
    1 can (8 ounces) water chestnuts, sliced
    ¼ cup pine nuts
    ¼ teaspoon thyme
    ¼ teaspoon ground ginger
       Salt and pepper to taste

Cook sprouts according to package directions; drain. In a large skillet, melt butter and sauté mushrooms, water chestnuts and pine nuts until lightly browned; add seasonings.(*) Combine sprouts with mushroom mixture and heat through.

Serves 4.

(*)May be prepared in advance to this point. Refrigerate up to 24 hours. To serve, proceed as directed above.

CABBAGE

ITALIAN CABBAGE SAUTE

- 2 tablespoons olive oil
- 1 large onion, chopped
- 1 head (about 1 pound) cabbage, washed and shredded
- 1 bay leaf
- 2 tablespoons cider vinegar
  Salt and pepper to taste

In a large skillet, heat oil and sauté onion until limp. Add cabbage and bay leaf. Cover and cook over medium heat until cabbage is tender, about 5 minutes. Add vinegar and boil rapidly, uncovered, until vinegar is absorbed. Season with salt and pepper.

Serves 4.

CABBAGE WITH CHINESE MUSHROOMS

- 1 medium head (about 1 pound) cabbage
- 4 dried Chinese mushrooms (buy in Chinese grocery)
- 2 tablespoons peanut oil
- ½ cup sliced bamboo shoots
- 1½ teaspoons salt

Wash cabbage and cut into 1-inch cubes. Soak mushrooms in warm water 20 minutes. Reserve ¼ cup mushroom water and dice mushrooms, discarding tough stems.

In a wok or large skillet, heat oil and stir-fry cabbage 2 minutes. Add bamboo shoots, mushrooms and salt; mix well. Add reserved mushroom water. Cover wok and cook 2 to 3 minutes over medium heat. Serve immediately.

Serves 4.

ROLLED CABBAGE

- Tomato Sauce (below)
- 1 medium head (about 1 pound) cabbage
- 1 pound ground beef
- 1 cup cooked rice
- 1 clove garlic, crushed
- 1 onion, finely chopped
- 2 tablespoons minced parsley
- 1 teaspoon salt
  Dash pepper
- ⅛ teaspoon cayenne pepper

Prepare Tomato Sauce. Wash cabbage and place in boiling salted water to cover; reduce heat, cover and simmer until soft, about 15 minutes. Drain, cool and cut out thick center spine. Remove leaves carefully.

Combine remaining ingredients and place a generous spoonful of the mixture on each leaf. Fold the leaves around the filling to make a package. Secure with toothpicks. Place rolls in a 1-quart casserole, folded sides down. Spoon Tomato Sauce over rolls. Cover and bake at 350° for 1 hour.(*)

Serves 4 as a main dish.

Tomato Sauce

- 2 tablespoons butter
- 1 clove garlic, crushed
- 2 onions, chopped
- 4 cups quartered whole tomatoes
- ½ cup beef broth
- ½ cup light brown sugar
- 1 tablespoon tarragon vinegar
- 2 tablespoons lemon juice
- 1½ teaspoons salt
- ¼ teaspoon pepper
- 1 bay leaf
- ¼ teaspoon thyme
- 1 teaspoon caraway seeds
- ½ cup seedless raisins

In a large skillet, melt butter and sauté garlic and onion until golden. Add remaining ingredients, cover and simmer 10 minutes.

(*)May be refrigerated up to 72 hours or frozen. To serve, bring to room temperature and reheat at 350° for 20 to 30 minutes, basting frequently with sauce.

GERMAN-STYLE RED CABBAGE

    3 tablespoons butter
    1 onion, chopped
    1 medium head (about 1 pound) red cabbage,
        finely shredded
    ½ cup water
    2 tablespoons wine vinegar
    4 cooking apples, peeled and sliced
    4 whole cloves
    1 bay leaf
    1 teaspoon salt
    1 tablespoon sugar
    3 tablespoons dry red wine

In a large skillet, melt butter and cook onion until golden brown. Add cabbage and continue cooking until cabbage is lightly browned. Stir in water, vinegar, apples, cloves, bay leaf and salt. Cover and simmer until cabbage is tender, about 45 minutes. Add sugar and wine and simmer 5 minutes longer.(*)

Serves 8.

(*)May be refrigerated up to 24 hours. To serve, reheat.

CHOCOLATE CAKE SURPRISE

    ½ cup butter
    1½ cups sugar
    3 eggs
    1 teaspoon vanilla
    2 cups flour
    1 teaspoon baking powder
    1 teaspoon baking soda
    ¼ teaspoon salt
    ½ cup cocoa powder
    1 cup water
    1 can (8 ounces) sauerkraut, drained,
        rinsed and chopped
    Sour Cream Chocolate Frosting (below)

Cream butter and sugar. Beat in eggs, one at a time; add vanilla. Sift dry ingredients together and add to creamed mixture alternately with water, beating after each addition. Fold in sauerkraut. Spoon into a greased and floured 13 x 9 x 2-inch baking pan. Bake at 350° for 35 to 40 minutes or until cake tests done. Cool in pan.

Frost with Sour Cream Chocolate Frosting.(*) Cut into squares.

Serves 12.

Sour Cream Chocolate Frosting

    1 package (6 ounces) semisweet chocolate bits
    ¼ cup butter
    ½ cup sour cream
    1 teaspoon vanilla
    ¼ teaspoon salt
    2½ cups sifted confectioners' sugar

Melt chocolate bits and butter in top of a double boiler over boiling water. Remove from heat and blend in sour cream, vanilla and salt. Gradually stir in confectioners' sugar and beat well until frosting is of spreading consistency.

(*)May be refrigerated up to 48 hours or frozen. To serve, bring to room temperature.

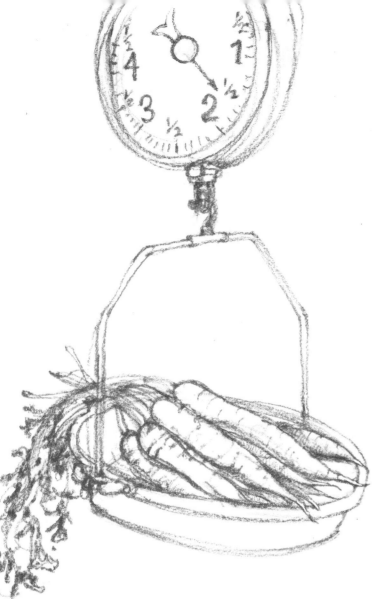

CARROTS

COLD CARROT SOUP

  4 cups chicken broth
  1 pound raw carrots, scraped
     and cut up
  ½ cup sliced celery
  1 cup light cream
  ½ teaspoon salt
  ¼ teaspoon pepper
  ½ teaspoon Worcestershire sauce

Bring chicken broth to a boil; reduce heat, cover and simmer carrots and celery until soft, about 30 minutes. Cool and puree in a blender or food processor until smooth. Refrigerate until well chilled (may be refrigerated up to 24 hours). When ready to serve, add cream and seasonings. Serve icy cold.

Serves 6.

CARROT-FRUIT SALAD

  1 cup pineapple juice
  1 package (3 ounces) orange gelatin
  3 tablespoons lemon juice
  ½ cup orange juice
  2 cups grated raw carrots
  ½ cup orange sections
  ½ teaspoon salt

Heat pineapple juice and dissolve gelatin in it. Stir in lemon and orange juices. Chill until mixture begins to thicken. Fold in carrots, orange sections and salt. Pour into a 1-quart mold and chill until firm (may be refrigerated up to 48 hours). Unmold and serve on greens.

Serves 6.

CARROT SLAW

  ½ cup sour cream
  ¼ cup milk
  1 tablespoon lemon juice
  1 teaspoon sugar
  ½ teaspoon salt
    Dash white pepper
  6 raw carrots, scraped and coarsely grated
    (about 3 cups)
  ½ cup chopped pitted dates
  ¼ cup slivered blanched almonds
    Chopped parsley

To prepare dressing, combine sour cream, milk, lemon juice, sugar, salt and pepper; mix well.

Combine carrots, dates and almonds. Pour dressing over carrot mixture, toss and chill (may be refrigerated up to 24 hours). When ready to serve, sprinkle with parsley.

Serves 6.

CARROTS AND ZUCCHINI

  1 bag (1 pound, 4 ounces) frozen
    whole baby carrots
  1 pound small zucchini, thickly sliced
  ½ teaspoon salt
  ½ teaspoon sugar
  1 teaspoon thyme
  1 tablespoon butter
    Dash pepper

Place carrots and zucchini in boiling water just to cover. Add salt, sugar and thyme. Cover, reduce heat and simmer until tender, about 10 minutes. Drain and add butter and pepper.

Serves 6.

CARROT-POTATO PUDDING

¾ cup grated carrots
2 cups grated potatoes
½ cup grated onion
½ teaspoon salt
¼ teaspoon pepper
½ cup flour
3 tablespoons chicken fat, melted
   (or vegetable oil)
2 eggs, beaten
1 tablespoon grated lemon rind

Combine grated vegetables. Add salt, pepper and flour and stir in melted chicken fat. Add eggs and lemon rind. Spread evenly in a 13 x 9 x 2-inch baking pan and bake at 375° until browned, 35 to 45 minutes.(*) Cut into individual serving pieces.

Serves 6.

(*)May be refrigerated up to 24 hours or frozen. To serve, bring to room temperature; reheat at 350° for 20 minutes.

GREAT GRANDMA'S TZIMMES

2 cups flour
2 teaspoons salt
¼ teaspoon pepper
½ cup chicken fat, melted
2 pounds raw carrots, cut into
   ½-inch slices
4 large sweet potatoes, peeled and
   cut into 1-inch slices
½ cup light brown sugar
¾ teaspoon ground ginger
1½ teaspoons salt
½ pound pitted prunes
2 teaspoons cornstarch mixed with
   2 tablespoons water

Prepare dumplings by combining flour, 2 teaspoons salt, pepper and chicken fat and forming into 8 balls.

In a large flameproof casserole, combine remaining ingredients except cornstarch mixture; add enough water to cover. Gently add dumplings and bring to a boil. Cover and simmer 1 hour. Pour cornstarch mixture down one side of the casserole in order not to disturb the dumplings. Cover and bake at 350° for 1 hour.(*)

Serves 10.

(*)May be refrigerated up to 24 hours. To serve, reheat at 350°.

MARINATED CARROTS WITH WALNUTS

1 pound raw carrots
1 cup white wine
1 cup chicken broth
5 tablespoons olive oil
3 tablespoons white wine vinegar
2 shallots, minced
1 clove garlic
1 teaspoon sugar
1 teaspoon salt
  Pepper
  Bouquet garni (parsley, bay leaf, thyme)
½ cup walnut halves
2 tablespoons olive oil

Scrape and cut carrots into ¼-inch strips, 2 inches long. Combine remaining ingredients except walnuts and 2 tablespoons oil. Bring to a boil, reduce heat and simmer 5 minutes. Add carrots and cook 5 minutes longer; cool. Marinate at least 24 hours in refrigerator (may be refrigerated up to 72 hours).

When ready to serve, blanch walnuts in boiling water 2 minutes; drain. Brown in 2 tablespoons oil. Drain carrots and toss with walnuts.

Serves 4.

SWEET-AND-SOUR CARROTS

2 pounds raw carrots
2 tablespoons butter, melted
2 tablespoons flour
  Salt and pepper to taste
1 tablespoon light brown sugar
1 cup hot water
3 tablespoons lemon juice
  Minced parsley

Scrape and quarter carrots. Drop into boiling salted water; reduce heat, cover and simmer until tender, 5 to 10 minutes. Drain.

In a saucepan, blend butter, flour, salt and pepper. Combine sugar, water and lemon juice; gradually stir into flour paste. Cook sauce until smooth and slightly thickened. Pour sauce over carrots and sprinkle with parsley.(*)

Serves 6.

(*)May be refrigerated up to 24 hours. To serve, reheat.

CARROT CAKE

   2 cups light brown sugar
1½ cups vegetable oil
   4 eggs
2¼ cups flour
   1 teaspoon salt
   1 teaspoon baking soda
   2 teaspoons baking powder
   2 teaspoons cinnamon
   3 cups grated raw carrots
   1 cup chopped walnuts
     Cream Cheese Frosting (below)

In a mixer bowl, combine sugar, oil and eggs. Beat 2 minutes on medium speed. Combine dry ingredients and add to sugar mixture. Beat 1 minute. Stir in grated carrots and nuts.

Spread batter in a greased and floured 10-inch tube pan and bake at 350° until cake tests done, about 1 hour. When cool, remove from pan.(*) Frost with Cream Cheese Frosting.

Serves 10.

Cream Cheese Frosting

   2 packages (3 ounces each) cream cheese
   3 tablespoons butter
   2 cups confectioners' sugar
   1 teaspoon vanilla

Soften cream cheese and butter. Combine with sugar and vanilla and beat until smooth and spreadable.

(*)May be refrigerated up to 48 hours or frozen, frosted or unfrosted.

CARROT CUSTARD PIE

   3 tablespoons butter
 ¾ cup sugar
   2 tablespoons flour
   3 eggs
1¼ cups heavy cream
1¼ cups grated raw carrots
 ½ teaspoon cinnamon
     Unbaked 9-inch pie crust

In a mixer bowl, cream butter and sugar. Add flour and beat well. Add eggs, one at a time, beating well. Pour in cream. Add carrots and cinnamon and mix well. Spoon into unbaked crust. Bake at 425° for 15 minutes; reduce heat to 350° and bake until firm, 25 to 30 minutes.(*)

Serves 8.

(*)May be refrigerated up to 24 hours or frozen. To serve, bring to room temperature.

HAWAIIAN CARROT BREAD

   2 cups flour
   2 teaspoons baking soda
   2 teaspoons cinnamon
 ½ teaspoon salt
   1 cup chopped walnuts
   1 cup vegetable oil
   2 teaspoons vanilla
1½ cups sugar
   2 cups coarsely grated raw carrots
   3 eggs, lightly beaten
   1 cup raisins
   1 cup shredded coconut

Sift flour, baking soda, cinnamon and salt together. Make a well in center of this mixture and mix in remaining ingredients. Pour into well-greased 9 x 5 x 3-inch loaf pan. Let stand 20 minutes before baking. Bake at 350° for 1 hour and 20 minutes. (*) Cool before slicing.

Serves 8.

(*)May be prepared in advance to this point. Refrigerate up to 48 hours or freeze. To serve, bring to room temperature.

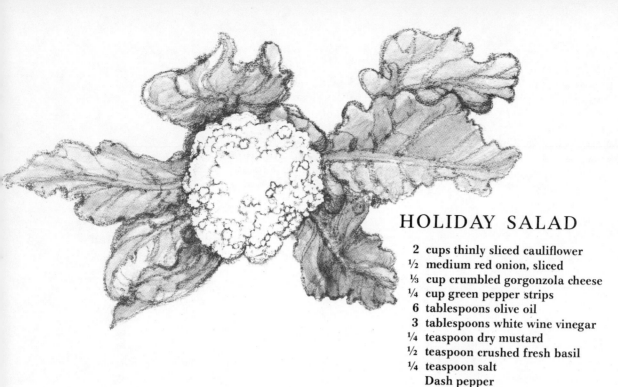

HOLIDAY SALAD

    2 cups thinly sliced cauliflower
    ½ medium red onion, sliced
    ⅓ cup crumbled gorgonzola cheese
    ¼ cup green pepper strips
    6 tablespoons olive oil
    3 tablespoons white wine vinegar
    ¼ teaspoon dry mustard
    ½ teaspoon crushed fresh basil
    ¼ teaspoon salt
       Dash pepper
    1 large bunch watercress

Combine (in a glass bowl, if possible) cauliflower, onion, cheese and pepper strips.

To prepare dressing, shake remaining ingredients except watercress in a jar. Pour dressing over vegetable mixture and toss to coat. Cover and refrigerate overnight (may be refrigerated up to 24 hours). When ready to serve, toss with watercress.

Serves 6.

CAULIFLOWER

Cauliflower may be served any number of ways. Raw and broken into flowerets, it makes a crunchy appetizer for a variety of dips. Whole or in flowerets, it can be boiled or steamed — and, if you like, the flowerets sautéed.

To cook a medium-size whole cauliflower (one will serve four), first trim off the tough stalk and the outer leaves; then make a few slashes in the remaining stalk. Place the head in a small amount of boiling salted water; reduce heat, cover and simmer about 12 minutes or until just tender. A slice of bread placed over the cauliflower during cooking will help to absorb its "cabbagey" smell.

If you wish to steam cauliflower, place the head on a trivet in a pan of water with the top of the trivet above the water level. Cover and steam about 20 minutes.

To serve a whole cauliflower, surround the head with a colorful vegetable like peas or carrots or a combination of the two. Or pour a tangy cheese sauce all over the head.

I like to take boiled flowerets and sauté them in a mixture of butter and vegetable oil seasoned with a bit of garlic.

CAULIFLOWER SLAW

    1   large head cauliflower, thinly sliced
    1   cup thinly sliced radishes
    1   small onion, grated
    ½   cup snipped watercress
    ¾   teaspoon salt
        Dash pepper
    1   cup sour cream
    1   envelope (0.7 ounces) dry garlic-cheese
          salad dressing mix
    1½ tablespoons lemon juice
    ¾   teaspoon seasoned salt
    2   tablespoons vegetable oil

Combine vegetables, ¾ teaspoon salt and the pepper.

To prepare dressing, combine sour cream with remaining ingredients; mix well. Pour dressing over vegetables and toss. Chill well (may be refrigerated up to 24 hours).

Serves 6.

JEANIE'S GIARDINIERA

- 1 small head cauliflower, cut into flowerets
- 6 carrots, cut into 2-inch strips
- 6 stalks celery, cut on bias into 1-inch pieces
- 2 green peppers, cut into 2-inch strips
- 1 teaspoon oregano
- ½ teaspoon pepper
- 1 jar (6 or 7 ounces) stuffed olives, drained
- 1½ cups wine vinegar
- ½ cup olive oil
- ½ cup water
- 4 tablespoons sugar
- 2 teaspoons salt

In a large saucepan, combine all ingredients and bring to a boil; reduce heat, cover and simmer 5 minutes. Cool and refrigerate at least overnight before serving (may be refrigerated up to 72 hours).

About 2 quarts.

CAULIFLOWER WITH HERB DRESSING

- 1 large head cauliflower
- 2 tablespoons butter
- 2 tablespoons flour
- 1 cup milk
- 2 tablespoons chopped fresh dill
- 1 tablespoon chopped fresh parsley
- ½ teaspoon grated onion
- ¼ teaspoon salt
- ½ cup sour cream or yogurt

Wash and trim cauliflower. Cook, covered, in 1 inch boiling salted water 15 to 20 minutes, until tender.

In a small saucepan, combine butter and flour. Gradually add milk; heat, stirring until smooth and boiling. Add dill, parsley, onion and salt. Lower heat and stir in sour cream; just heat through. To serve, place cauliflower on a serving platter and top with sauce.

Serves 6.

CAULIFLOWER WITH CIDER SAUCE

- 1 medium head cauliflower
- 1 tablespoon butter
- 1 tablespoon flour
- ⅓ cup apple cider
- ⅓ cup heavy cream
- ¼ teaspoon salt
- ¼ teaspoon pumpkin pie spice
- 1 tablespoon chutney

Wash cauliflower and break off heavy leaves and reserve. In a pot large enough to hold the cauliflower, bring 1 inch of salted water to a boil. Place reserved cauliflower leaves on bottom and set cauliflower on leaves. Cover and steam for 15 to 20 minutes, until tender; drain well.

To prepare sauce, melt butter in top of a double boiler. Stir in flour, then whip in cider and heavy cream. Add salt and cook until thickened, about 15 minutes. Stir in pumpkin pie spice and chutney. Pour sauce over cauliflower and serve immediately.

Serves 4.

CELERY

Too many people think of celery only as a "raw" vegetable. If you fall into that group, you really do owe it to yourself to try it braised. Either the stalks, cut into slices, or the hearts, cut in half, are delicious. You can sauté them first in butter and then add a small amount of water or bouillon; cover and simmer until crisp-tender. Or, you can drop the slices or hearts into boiling salted water and simmer. The timing depends on the size of the slices, but test after 5 minutes. Serve with butter or a cream sauce.

CELERY LIPTAUER

  1 cup creamed cottage cheese
½ cup soft butter
1½ teaspoons dry mustard
1½ teaspoons caraway seeds
1½ teaspoons chopped chives
1½ teaspoons capers
  2 teaspoons minced anchovies
24 stalks celery, cut into 3- to 4-inch pieces
    Paprika
    Chopped parsley

Mix cottage cheese and butter. Add mustard, caraway seeds, chives, capers and anchovies; mix well. Stuff mixture into celery stalks and sprinkle with paprika and chopped parsley.

About 48 hors d'oeuvres.

FIONA'S WINTER SALAD

¾ cup julienne strips Gruyère cheese
  2 cups finely chopped celery
½ pound fresh mushrooms, sliced
½ cup minced parsley
  1 teaspoon Dijon-type mustard
  3 tablespoons olive oil
  1 tablespoon wine vinegar
½ teaspoon sugar
½ teaspoon salt
¼ teaspoon pepper

Combine the cheese, celery, mushrooms and parsley.

To prepare dressing, combine remaining ingredients and beat well with a fork or whisk. When ready to serve, pour dressing over salad, toss and let stand 15 minutes to blend flavors.

Serves 6.

ALMOND BAKED CELERY

  1 bunch celery, without leaves, thinly sliced
½ cup chopped blanched almonds, toasted
½ cup grated sharp Cheddar cheese
  1 teaspoon salt
⅛ teaspoon pepper
½ teaspoon paprika
  2 cans (10¾ ounces each) cream of celery soup
½ cup dry bread crumbs
    Melted butter

Place celery in a buttered 1-quart casserole; cover with nuts and sprinkle with cheese. Combine seasonings with soup and pour over all. Top with bread crumbs and drizzle with melted butter.(*) Bake, uncovered, at 375° for 40 to 45 minutes.

Serves 6.

(*)May be prepared in advance to this point. Refrigerate up to 24 hours. To serve, bring to room temperature and bake as directed above.

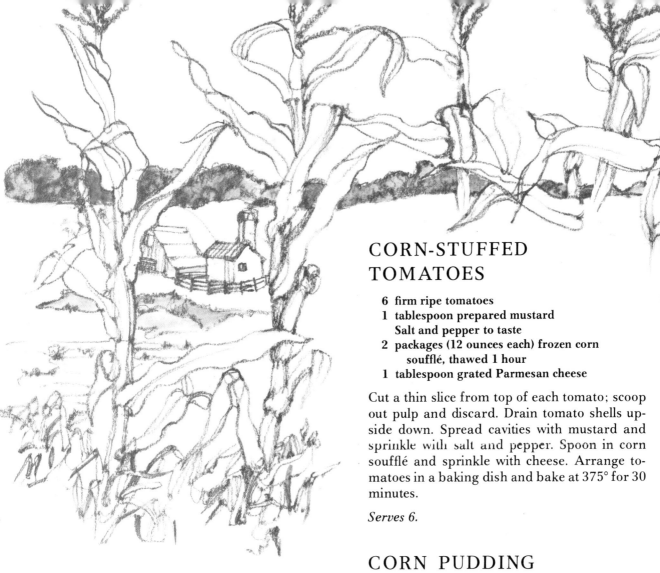

CORN-STUFFED TOMATOES

  6 firm ripe tomatoes
  1 tablespoon prepared mustard
    Salt and pepper to taste
  2 packages (12 ounces each) frozen corn
      soufflé, thawed 1 hour
  1 tablespoon grated Parmesan cheese

Cut a thin slice from top of each tomato; scoop out pulp and discard. Drain tomato shells upside down. Spread cavities with mustard and sprinkle with salt and pepper. Spoon in corn soufflé and sprinkle with cheese. Arrange tomatoes in a baking dish and bake at 375° for 30 minutes.

Serves 6.

CORN PUDDING ESPAGNOLE

  ½ green pepper, diced
  1 tablespoon butter
  1 can (16½ ounces) cream-style corn
  1 can (8 ounces) whole kernel corn, drained
  2 tablespoons pimiento, diced
  ½ medium onion, grated
  ¼ cup light cream
  4 eggs, beaten
  1 teaspoon salt
  ¼ teaspoon pepper
  2 tablespoons sugar
  2 tablespoons minced parsley
    Pinch basil

Sauté green pepper in butter until soft. Turn into a 2-quart casserole and stir in remaining ingredients.(*) Bake, uncovered, at 375° until firm in center and lightly browned on top, about 45 minutes.

Serves 6.

(*)May be prepared in advance to this point. Refrigerate up to 24 hours. To serve, bring to room temperature and bake as directed above.

CORN

At the risk of seeming rigid, I must confess that I feel there is an unbreakable rule when it comes to preparing corn on the cob: It must be freshly picked and cooked within an hour of picking to be at its best. Admittedly, it is difficult to grow your own corn; but when it is in season, it is usually abundantly available at farmers' markets, hopefully nearby. I never buy fresh corn out of season and, even in season, I never buy it in the supermarket.

To prepare, simply remove the husks and silk from the ears. Drop them in boiling water, to which you have added salt and a pinch of sugar. Boil, uncovered, 8 to 10 minutes and serve immediately with melted butter, salt and pepper.

CUCUMBERS

CUCUMBER-RADISH CANAPES

    12 thin slices white bread
     2 tablespoons mayonnaise
     1 clove garlic, crushed
    ½ teaspoon dill weed
     1 cucumber, thinly sliced
    ½ cup Sausalito French Dressing (below)
        Salt
    12 radishes, thinly sliced
        Minced parsley

Cut 2 rounds from each bread slice with cookie cutter. Spread each round with mayonnaise mixed with garlic and dill.

Marinate sliced cucumber in Sausalito French Dressing at least 1 hour. Place 1 slice of cucumber on each bread round. Sprinkle with salt. Top with thin slices of radish and sprinkle with parsley.(*)

2 dozen canapés.

Sausalito French Dressing

    1½ cups olive oil
     ½ cup wine vinegar
      1 tablespoon salt
     ⅛ teaspoon pepper
     ¼ teaspoon paprika
      3 tablespoons sugar
      3 tablespoons catsup
      1 teaspoon chili sauce
      1 teaspoon lemon juice
     ½ teaspoon prepared mustard
     ½ teaspoon prepared horseradish
         Dash hot pepper sauce

Combine all ingredients in a jar and shake vigorously. Dressing will keep almost indefinitely in the refrigerator.

About 2 cups.

(*)May be refrigerated up to 24 hours. To keep in the refrigerator, cover with waxed paper, then with a damp towel.

PERSIAN CUCUMBER DIP

     1 cup unflavored yogurt
     1 small onion, grated
     1 small cucumber, peeled and diced
    ¼ cup raisins
    ¼ cup chopped fresh mint leaves
        Salt to taste
     1 pound pita bread (Middle Eastern flat bread)

Combine all ingredients except pita bread and chill (may be refrigerated up to 72 hours).

Cut pita bread into triangles and toast under broiler; use as dippers.

2 cups.

CUCUMBER SALAD

     2 medium cucumbers
    ½ teaspoon salt
     1 teaspoon soy sauce
     1 tablespoon sugar
     1 tablespoon white vinegar
     2 teaspoons sesame oil

Peel cucumbers and cut in half lengthwise. Remove seeds from center of each half and cut into ¼-inch slices.

To prepare dressing, combine remaining ingredients. Toss dressing with cucumbers.

Serves 4.

QUICKLES

     3 large cucumbers, peeled and sliced
     3 large onions, thinly sliced
    ¼ cup coarse salt
     1 cup cider vinegar
     1 cup sugar
    ½ cup water
    ¼ cup dill seeds

Layer cucumber and onion slices in a large bowl, sprinkling each layer with coarse salt. Place ice cubes on top of mixture and press down with a plate. Refrigerate 12 to 24 hours.

At least 2 hours before serving, bring remaining ingredients to a boil; reduce heat, cover and simmer 5 minutes. Squeeze the salted ice water from the cucumber and onion mixture. Place vegetables in a bowl and pour in vinegar mixture, straining out dill seeds. Refrigerate until ready to serve (may be refrigerated up to 1 week).

2 quarts.

WALTER'S PICKLES

4 quarts pickle-size cucumbers (2 to 3
    inches long)
5 quarts water
⅓ cup cider vinegar
½ cup salt
2½ teaspoons alum
5 green peppers, cut into 1-inch squares
3 garlic buds, broken into cloves
3 to 4 bunches fresh dill, cut into sprigs

Scrub cucumbers and soak overnight in salted water. (The bathtub — don't laugh — is perfect for this.) Dry each one and feel for soft spots and bruises. Discard any cucumbers that are less than perfect.

Prepare a brine solution by combining the water, vinegar and salt. Bring to a boil and keep at the boiling point.

Sterilize 1-quart jars. In bottom of each jar, place a pinch of alum, 4 or 5 pieces of green pepper, 3 cloves of garlic and a few sprigs of dill. (If you cannot get fresh dill, you may use dried dill weed.) Squeeze the cukes into the jars in an upright position. Add more dill, stems and all. Add more garlic, if desired. Fill jars to the top with boiling brine. Cap jars with sterilized tops and seal.

Let stand at least 2 weeks. If you keep some of the pickles in the refrigerator, they will stay crisp for a while without processing, but they tend to get soft after long periods. They will keep indefinitely after processing.

15 to 20 quarts.

CUCUMBER MOUSSE

2 large cucumbers
2 teaspoons salt
½ teaspoon sugar
¼ cup white vinegar
1 cup cold water
3 envelopes unflavored gelatin
2 tablespoons chopped fresh mint leaves
2 slices onion, coarsley chopped
⅓ cup chopped parsley
1 cup sour cream
½ cup mayonnaise
¼ teaspoon hot pepper sauce
    Cucumber slices and mint leaves

Peel, seed and dice cucumbers and sprinkle with 1 teaspoon of the salt and the sugar. Let stand 20 minutes.

In a saucepan, combine vinegar and water; sprinkle gelatin on it to soften. Stir over low heat to dissolve gelatin. Remove from heat and add remaining salt and the mint.

In a blender or food processor, puree cucumber, onion and parsley; add to gelatin mixture. Refrigerate until slightly thickened. Beat in sour cream and mayonnaise. Season with hot pepper sauce. Pour into a 1-quart mold and chill until firm, at least 3 hours (may be refrigerated up to 48 hours).

When ready to serve, unmold onto chilled plate and decorate with cucumber slices and mint leaves.

Serves 6.

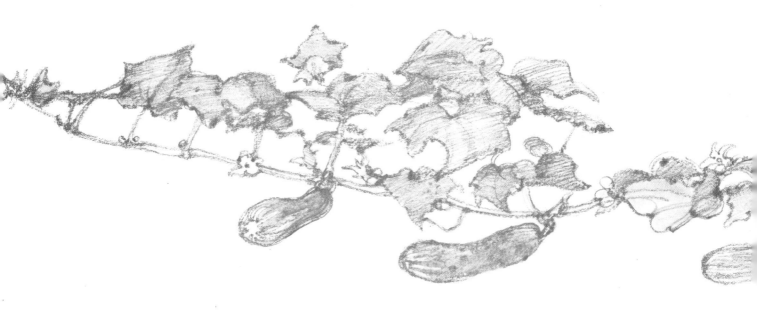

EGGPLANT

JAPANESE EGGPLANT HORS D'OEUVRE

    1 small eggplant
    ¼ teaspoon salt
    2 tablespoons vinegar
    2 tablespoons sugar
    2 tablespoons corn oil
    2 teaspoons Japanese soy sauce

Peel eggplant and cut into julienne strips. Salt eggplant and let stand 15 minutes; then squeeze out liquid. Boil remaining ingredients until sugar is dissolved. Pour sauce over eggplant and chill at least 2 hours (may be refrigerated up to 48 hours). Serve with toothpicks.

About 2 cups.

EGGPLANT AND YOGURT DIP

    1 medium eggplant
    1 teaspoon minced onion
    1 teaspoon lemon juice
    1 cup unflavored yogurt
      Salt to taste
    3 tablespoons butter
    1 large onion, thinly sliced
    1 pound pita bread (Middle Eastern flat bread)

Place eggplant on a sheet of aluminum foil and bake at 350° for 1 hour; cool. Cut eggplant in half lengthwise and scrape pulp into a mixing bowl. Chop well and mix in minced onion, lemon juice, yogurt and salt. Blend well and chill (may be refrigerated up to 24 hours).

When ready to serve, heat butter in a skillet and cook onion slices until golden brown. Spoon the onions over eggplant. Cut pita bread into triangles and toast under broiler; use as dippers.

About 2 cups.

COLD EGGPLANT SOUP

    1 tablespoon butter
    1 onion, sliced
    1 teaspoon curry powder
1½ pounds eggplant, peeled and cubed
    5 cups chicken broth
 ½ cup sour cream

Melt butter and sauté onion until limp. Add curry powder and cook 2 minutes longer. Add eggplant and chicken broth. Bring to a boil; reduce heat, cover and simmer 45 minutes. Cool. Puree eggplant mixture in a blender or food processor; chill (may be refrigerated up to 48 hours or frozen). When ready to serve, garnish with dollops of sour cream.

Serves 6.

EGGPLANT SZECHWAN

    1 small eggplant
      Salt
 ¼ pound pork (1 pork chop)
    2 to 3 tablespoons finely chopped gingerroot
 ¼ cup finely chopped garlic
    1 tablespoon hot bean sauce (buy in
        Chinese grocery)
    2 tablespoons dark soy sauce
    1 teaspoon salt
    1 teaspoon sugar
 ½ cup chicken broth
    6 tablespoons peanut oil
    2 green onions, chopped
    2 teaspoons sesame oil
    1 tablespoon cornstarch mixed with
        2 tablespoons water

Peel eggplant and cut into strips 3 inches long and as thick as your little finger. Salt lightly; after 5 minutes, pat dry. Cut pork into small pieces. Mix gingerroot and garlic (chopped as fine as possible) with hot bean sauce. Mix soy sauce, salt, sugar and chicken broth.

In a wok or large skillet, heat 3 tablespoons of the peanut oil and stir-fry eggplant until soft and moist. Remove from wok and drain excess oil.

Heat remaining peanut oil and stir-fry meat until it loses its color. Add gingerroot, garlic and hot bean sauce; stir-fry. Add soy sauce mixture and eggplant. Cook until liquid starts to disappear. Add green onions and sesame oil. Stir in cornstarch paste and cook a few minutes, just until sauce thickens.

Serves 4.

CRUSTY EGGPLANT

    2 medium eggplants
    2 eggs
 ¼ cup freshly grated Parmesan cheese
 ½ cup dry bread crumbs
    1 tablespoon chopped parsley
 ¼ teaspoon salt
 ⅛ teaspoon pepper
 ¼ cup flour
 ¼ cup butter, melted

Peel eggplants and slice into ½-inch-thick rounds. Beat eggs in a shallow bowl.

In a similar bowl, combine cheese, bread crumbs, parsley, salt and pepper. Dust each eggplant slice with flour, then dip in egg, then in crumb mixture. Pour half the butter into each of 2 baking pans, 15 x 10 x 1 inch, coating bottoms evenly. Arrange eggplant slices in butter.(*) Bake at 400° for 25 minutes, turning once to brown both sides.

Serves 6.

(*)May be prepared in advance to this point. Refrigerate up to 24 hours. To serve, bring to room temperature and bake as directed above.

CREAMY
EGGPLANT CUSTARD

    1 large eggplant
    4 eggs
    1 cup light cream
 ¼ cup butter, melted
 ½ teaspoon salt
 ⅛ teaspoon pepper
 ¼ teaspoon dill weed
 ¼ cup finely chopped parsley

Peel eggplant and cut into 1-inch cubes. Put eggplant in boiling salted water, reduce heat, cover and simmer until tender, about 8 minutes. Drain well and mash. Add remaining ingredients and beat until light and fluffy. Pour into a 2-quart casserole.(*) Bake, uncovered, at 350° 35 minutes or until set.

Serves 6.

(*)May be prepared in advance to this point. Refrigerate up to 24 hours. To serve, bring to room temperature and bake as directed above.

STUFFED EGGPLANT

  2 medium eggplants
½ cup vegetable oil
  2 tomatoes, peeled and chopped
  1 cup chopped onion
  1 clove garlic, crushed
¼ cup chopped parsley
¼ cup chopped green onions
  1 cup cooked rice (⅓ cup raw)
  8 ounces small-curd cottage cheese or
      feta cheese
      Salt and pepper to taste
½ teaspoon oregano
½ teaspoon thyme
¼ cup dry seasoned bread crumbs

Cut eggplants in half lengthwise; remove centers, leaving ½-inch-thick shells. Dice pulp.

In a large skillet, heat oil and sauté pulp until soft. Add tomatoes, onion, garlic, parsley and green onions. Heat, stirring, until vegetables are tender, 5 minutes. Stir in cooked rice, cheese and seasonings. Stuff eggplant shells with mixture. Sprinkle tops with seasoned bread crumbs.(*)

Place stuffed shells in a shallow baking pan with just enough water to cover base of pan. Bake at 350° for 35 to 40 minutes.

Serves 4 as a main dish.

(*)May be prepared in advance to this point. Refrigerate up to 24 hours. To serve, bring to room temperature and bake as directed above.

CHEDDAR-STUFFED EGGPLANT

  2 medium eggplants
  2 cups grated sharp Cheddar cheese
  1 onion, finely chopped
  3 slices soft white bread, cubed
  2 tablespoons chopped parsley
  2 tablespoons chopped chives
  2 eggs, separated
      Salt and pepper to taste
  2 tablespoons butter
  2 tablespoons flour
  1 cup milk

Cut eggplants in half horizontally and scoop out pulp. Cover and cook pulp with a little water until tender, about 20 minutes; mash. Add cheese, onion, bread, parsley, chives, egg yolks and salt and pepper.

In a large saucepan, melt butter and gradually stir in flour. Gradually add milk, stirring until

thickened. Stir into eggplant mixture and fold in stiffly beaten egg whites. Spoon into eggplant shells. Bake on a foil-covered cookie sheet at 350° for 40 minutes or until tops brown.(*)

Serves 4 as a main dish.

(*)May be refrigerated up to 24 hours or frozen. To serve, bring to room temperature and reheat.

EGGPLANT QUICHE

      10-inch Pie Shell (below)
  1 medium eggplant
⅔ cup vegetable oil
      Salt and pepper to taste
  3 eggs, lightly beaten
  1 can (28 ounces) Italian tomatoes, drained
  2 teaspoons basil
  2 tablespoons minced parsley
¾ cup grated Swiss cheese

Prepare Pie Shell. Peel and dice eggplant. In a large skillet, heat oil and sauté eggplant 10 minutes; drain on paper towels. Season with salt and pepper; mix with eggs, tomatoes, basil and parsley.

Pour eggplant mixture into pie shell and sprinkle with grated Swiss cheese. Bake at 375° for 40 minutes.(*)

Serves 8 as a main dish.

Pie Shell

½ cup butter
1⅔ cups flour
      Pinch salt
  1 egg yolk
  1 tablespoon vegetable oil
¼ cup cold water
  1 tablespoon Dijon-type mustard
¾ cup grated Swiss cheese

Cut butter into flour and salt until mixture resembles oatmeal. Beat egg yolk with oil and water. Mix into flour and form into a ball. Refrigerate until firm. Roll out dough for a 10-inch pie plate. Spread mustard on pie shell and sprinkle with Swiss cheese.

(*)May be refrigerated up to 24 hours or frozen. To serve, bring to room temperature and reheat at 375° for 8 to 10 minutes.

EGGPLANT PIE

    1 medium eggplant, peeled and sliced
       ¼ inch thick
    ½ teaspoon salt
    ⅛ teaspoon pepper
    2 ripe tomatoes, sliced
    1 green pepper, sliced into rings
    1 small onion, thinly sliced
    2 tablespoons olive oil
    1 teaspoon minced garlic
    1 teaspoon basil
    ¼ teaspoon salt
    4 ounces mozzarella cheese, thinly sliced
    ½ cup grated Parmesan cheese

Arrange eggplant in a single layer on a foil-covered baking sheet; sprinkle with ½ teaspoon salt and the pepper. Broil 6 inches from heat until lightly browned, about 8 minutes.

Overlap eggplant slices, browned sides down, in a 10-inch pie plate. Arrange tomatoes, green pepper and onion over eggplant. Drizzle with oil and sprinkle with garlic, basil and ¼ teaspoon salt.(*) Bake at 375° for 25 minutes.

Arrange mozzarella cheese on top of pie and sprinkle with Parmesan cheese. Bake 15 minutes longer or until cheese is golden.

Serves 4 as a main dish.

(*)May be prepared in advance to this point. Refrigerate up to 24 hours. To serve, bring to room temperature and bake as directed above.

EGGPLANT SANDWICH

       Tomato Sauce (below)
    2 tablespoons butter
    1 onion, finely chopped
    ¼ pound fresh mushrooms, chopped
    2 pounds ground beef
    ½ cup dry bread crumbs
    3 egg yolks
    1½ teaspoons salt
    ¼ teaspoon pepper
       Dash sage
    8 slices provolone cheese
    1 large eggplant, cut into 16 thin slices
       Flour
    ½ cup vegetable oil
    ½ cup grated Parmesan cheese

Prepare Tomato Sauce. Melt butter and sauté onion until tender but not brown. Add mushrooms and cook 2 to 3 minutes. Combine this mixture with ground beef, bread crumbs, ⅓ cup of the Tomato Sauce, the egg yolks, salt, pepper and sage. Form into 16 patties and make 8 "sandwiches" with provolone slices between. Pinch edges together and broil 5 minutes on each side.

Salt eggplant slices and coat with flour. Heat oil and sauté eggplant slices until lightly browned. In a 13 x 9 x 2-inch baking dish, alternate layers of eggplant and meat-cheese "sandwiches." Top with remaining Tomato Sauce and sprinkle with grated Parmesan cheese.(*) Bake, uncovered, at 350° for 20 to 30 minutes, until bubbly and cheese is brown.

Serves 8 as a main dish.

Tomato Sauce

    4 cups canned tomatoes, with liquid
    1 cup tomato juice
    1 onion, sliced
    2 stalks celery, with leaves
    ¼ cup butter
    ¼ cup flour
    ½ teaspoon sugar
    ½ teaspoon salt
    ¼ teaspoon pepper

Combine tomatoes, juice, onion and celery. Simmer 15 minutes. Strain mixture and reserve liquid. Melt butter; stir in flour and gradually add reserved liquid. Season with sugar, salt and pepper. Cook, stirring, until slightly thickened.

(*)May be prepared in advance to this point. Refrigerate up to 24 hours or freeze. To serve, bring to room temperature and bake as directed above.

ENDIVE

ENDIVE PINWHEEL SALAD

    4 Belgian endives
    3 large tomatoes, cut into wedges
    2 cans (2 ounces each) anchovy fillets
    ¼ cup herbed salad dressing
      Freshly ground pepper

Crisp endives in ice water for at least 15 minutes before using. Dry gently with paper towels. Separate endive leaves and arrange pinwheel-fashion on a large round glass or china platter. Create an attractive pattern with the tomato wedges and anchovy fillets between leaves. Pour on dressing and grind pepper over all.

Serves 8.

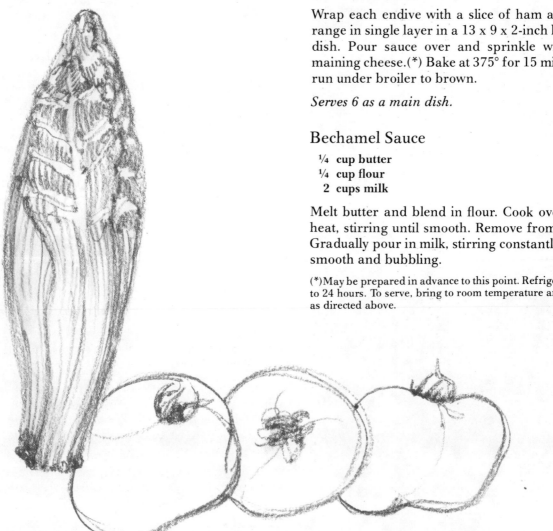

ENDIVE AND HAM AU GRATIN

    ¼ cup butter
    ½ teaspoon sugar
    12 Belgian endives
       Salt and pepper
       Bechamel Sauce (below)
    2 cups grated Gruyère cheese
    1 egg yolk
       Pinch nutmeg
       Salt and pepper to taste
    12 thin slices boiled ham

In a large skillet, melt butter and sprinkle in sugar. Add endives, 6 at a time, and roll them around to coat; sprinkle with salt and pepper. Cover endives with a buttered round of waxed paper; cover the skillet. Cook until tender, 10 to 15 minutes.

Prepare Bechamel Sauce; cool 5 minutes. Stir in 1⅓ cups of the cheese, the egg yolk, nutmeg and salt and pepper.

Wrap each endive with a slice of ham and arrange in single layer in a 13 x 9 x 2-inch baking dish. Pour sauce over and sprinkle with remaining cheese.(*) Bake at 375° for 15 minutes; run under broiler to brown.

Serves 6 as a main dish.

Bechamel Sauce

    ¼ cup butter
    ¼ cup flour
    2 cups milk

Melt butter and blend in flour. Cook over low heat, stirring until smooth. Remove from heat. Gradually pour in milk, stirring constantly until smooth and bubbling.

(*)May be prepared in advance to this point. Refrigerate up to 24 hours. To serve, bring to room temperature and bake as directed above.

ESCAROLE

ESCAROLE SOUP

  2 quarts chicken broth
  2 cups shredded escarole
  4 eggs
  ½ cup grated Parmesan cheese
  ¼ cup farina
  ¼ teaspoon nutmeg
  ½ teaspoon salt
  ¼ teaspoon pepper

In a large saucepan, bring broth to a boil. Add escarole, reduce heat, cover and simmer 5 to 10 minutes until escarole is limp. In a small bowl, combine eggs, cheese and farina. Beat into soup mixture and continue beating until thoroughly mixed in. Add seasonings. Return soup to a boil, reduce heat, cover and simmer 5 minutes longer.(*)

Serves 8.

(*)May be refrigerated up to 48 hours or frozen. To serve, reheat.

HERBED ESCAROLE

  2 pounds escarole
  ¼ cup olive oil
  2 cloves garlic, split
  ½ teaspoon oregano
1¼ teaspoons salt
  ¼ teaspoon freshly ground pepper
  ¼ cup pine nuts

Separate escarole leaves, discarding outer ones; wash and drain. Cut leaves into quarters.

In a large skillet, heat olive oil and brown garlic. Discard browned garlic. Add escarole and oregano. Cover and cook over medium heat until tender, 10 to 15 minutes. Season with salt and pepper. Toss with pine nuts.

Serves 4.

FENNEL

FENNEL AND AVOCADO VINAIGRETTE

- 1 large or 2 small bulbs fennel
- 1 tomato, peeled, seeded and cubed
- 1 can (2 ounces) rolled anchovy fillets
- 2 hard-boiled eggs, cut into wedges
- 1 ripe avocado
- 12 pitted black olives
- 3 tablespoons olive oil
- 1 tablespoon red wine vinegar
- 1 clove garlic, finely chopped
- ½ teaspoon oregano
  - Salt and pepper to taste

Trim tops and bases from fennel bulbs. Discard tough outer leaves. Cut remaining fennel lengthwise into ½-inch slices. Arrange slices in single layer on serving platter. Arrange tomato cubes and anchovies on top of fennel. Garnish platter with wedges of hard-boiled egg. Peel and slice avocado. Arrange avocado slices and olives around platter.

To prepare dressing, mix oil, vinegar, garlic, oregano, salt and pepper. Beat with a fork or whisk and pour over all.

Serves 6.

FENNEL AU GRATIN

- 3 large or 6 small bulbs fennel
- ¼ cup butter
  - Salt and pepper to taste
- 1 cup chicken broth
- ½ cup grated Parmesan cheese

Trim tops and bases from fennel bulbs. Discard tough outer leaves. Cut fennel bulbs in half or quarters, depending on their size. Drop fennel into boiling salted water to cover; reduce heat, cover and simmer until tender, 15 to 20 minutes. Drain and arrange cut side down in a 13 x 9 x 2-inch baking dish. Add salt, pepper and chicken broth. Sprinkle with grated cheese.(*) Bake at 400° for 30 minutes.

Serves 6.

(*)May be prepared in advance to this point. Refrigerate up to 24 hours. To serve, bring to room temperature and bake as directed above.

HEARTS OF PALM

HEARTS OF PALM SALAD

- Romaine lettuce leaves
- 1 can (14 ounces) hearts of palm
- ½ Bermuda onion, sliced
- 1 tomato, diced
  - Snipped fresh dill
- 1 tablespoon chopped chives
- 1 tablespoon chopped parsley
- 1 clove garlic, crushed
- 3 tablespoons mayonnaise
  - Juice of ½ lime
  - Salt and pepper to taste

Wash lettuce leaves, pat dry and arrange in a salad bowl. Drain hearts of palm, reserving 3 tablespoons of the liquid; slice and add to salad bowl with onion and tomato. Sprinkle with fresh herbs.

To prepare dressing, combine reserved hearts of palm liquid with remaining ingredients in a jar and shake until blended. Pour over salad.

Serves 6.

LETTUCE

JUDY'S OVERNIGHT SALAD

- 1 large head iceberg lettuce, shredded
- 1 package (10 ounces) frozen peas, thawed
- 2 tablespoons chopped green onions
- 2 tablespoons chopped green pepper
  Lemon pepper
- ¾ cup mayonnaise
- 2 tablespoons sugar
- 1 cup grated sharp Cheddar cheese
- 8 slices bacon, crisply cooked and crumbled

In a large salad bowl, combine lettuce, peas, green onions and green pepper. Sprinkle with lemon pepper. Cover entire top of salad with mayonnaise — do not stir. Sprinkle with sugar, cheese and bacon. Cover tightly with aluminum foil and refrigerate overnight (may be refrigerated up to 48 hours). Toss to serve.

Serves 8.

PAT'S FAR EAST SALAD

- 2 tablespoons vegetable oil
- 1½ teaspoons soy sauce
- 1 tablespoon wine vinegar
- ¼ teaspoon salt
- ¼ teaspoon ground ginger
  Dash pepper
- 2 heads Bibb lettuce, torn
- ½ head iceberg lettuce, shredded
- 1 Bermuda onion, sliced
- ½ pound fresh bean sprouts (or canned, if rinsed well)
- 1 can (11 ounces) mandarin oranges, drained

To prepare dressing, combine oil, soy sauce, vinegar, salt, ginger and pepper; shake well.

Combine remaining ingredients and toss with dressing.

Serves 6.

LETTUCE WITH CHINESE OYSTER SAUCE

- 1 head iceberg lettuce
- 1 can (15 ounces) straw mushrooms (buy in Chinese grocery)
- 2 tablespoons oyster sauce (buy in Chinese grocery)
- 1 tablespoon cornstarch
- 4 tablespoons peanut oil
- 1 teaspoon salt

Wash lettuce and cut into 1-inch cubes. Drain straw mushrooms, reserving ¼ cup mushroom liquid. Cut mushrooms in half. Mix oyster sauce, cornstarch and reserved mushroom liquid.

Heat a wok or large skillet; add 2 tablespoons of the oil and stir-fry lettuce 1 minute. Stir in salt, then remove lettuce to serving dish. Heat remaining oil in wok and stir-fry mushrooms 1 minute. Add reserved cornstarch mixture and mix well. Pour mixture over lettuce and serve immediately.

Serves 4.

MUSHROOMS

Mushrooms — preferably fresh, but canned if necessary — add a lovely touch to almost any dish. I like fresh mushrooms that are snowy white and brushed clean with a damp towel. If washed, mushrooms should be very thoroughly dried. Slice off the bottom of the stem if it is tough. Otherwise, use mushrooms whole, sliced or chopped — according to your recipe.

Raw mushrooms are terrific in salads. For a side dish, I like them sautéed in a little butter for 3 or 4 minutes or brushed lightly with butter or oil and broiled for no more than 2 minutes on each side.

PICKLED MUSHROOMS

  1 pound fresh mushrooms
  ⅔ cup boiling water
      Pinch salt
  ⅓ cup white vinegar
  2 whole cloves
 10 to 12 peppercorns
  1 bay leaf
  1 tablespoon sugar
  2 teaspoons salt

Wash mushrooms and drop into ⅔ cup boiling salted water; reduce heat, cover and simmer 6 to 7 minutes. Drain, reserving cooking liquid.

Combine remaining ingredients with reserved cooking liquid in a saucepan, cover and boil 6 minutes. Place mushrooms in a container and pour marinade over. Refrigerate until ready to serve (may be refrigerated up to 72 hours). Great hors d'oeuvres!

About 3 dozen.

STUFFED RAW MUSHROOM CAPS

 1 pound fresh mushrooms
 8 ounces blue cheese
 4 teaspoons light cream
 2 tablespoons chopped chives

Wash and dry mushrooms. Remove stems and chop enough to make ½ cup. Combine chopped stems with blue cheese, cream and chives. Fill mushroom caps with the mixture and chill (may be refrigerated up to 48 hours).

About 3 dozen.

HOT MUSHROOM MERINGUES

 2 tablespoons butter
 1 cup chopped fresh mushrooms
 ¼ teaspoon salt
    Pinch pepper
 ⅛ teaspoon garlic salt
 2 eggs, separated
 2 tablespoons heavy cream
 6 slices white bread
    Grated Parmesan cheese

Melt butter and sauté mushrooms 2 to 3 minutes. Season with salt, pepper and garlic salt. Combine egg yolks with cream; add to mushrooms. Cook over low heat until thickened, 2 to 3 minutes longer.

Remove crusts from bread; cut each slice in quarters. Toast one side. Spread mushroom mixture on untoasted side. Sprinkle with cheese. Beat egg whites until stiff. Cover mushroom mixture with egg whites. Bake on a greased cookie sheet at 400° for 10 to 15 minutes, until lightly browned.

About 2 dozen hors d'oeuvres.

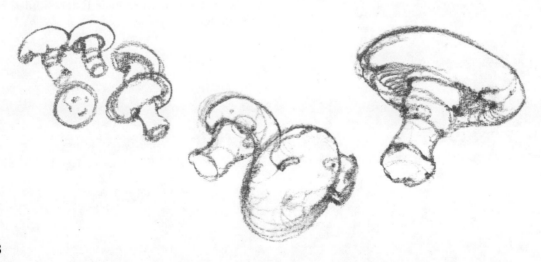

MUSHROOM SOUP

1½ pounds fresh mushrooms
3 tablespoons butter
3 tablespoons flour
8 cups chicken broth
¾ cup heavy cream

Wash, dry and slice mushrooms. In a large saucepan, melt butter and sauté mushrooms 5 to 6 minutes. Sprinkle with flour and cook 1 minute longer. Remove from heat and add 1 cup of the chicken broth; stir well. Add remaining broth, cover and simmer 10 minutes. Stir in cream and heat, but do not boil.(*)

Serves 8.

(*)May be refrigerated up to 24 hours or frozen. To serve, reheat.

MUSHROOM-ORANGE SALAD

¼ cup slivered almonds
4 slices bacon
1 large head lettuce
1 can (11 ounces) mandarin oranges, drained
½ pound fresh mushrooms, sliced
6 tablespoons vegetable oil
3 tablespoons white wine vinegar
3 tablespoons crumbled blue cheese
¼ teaspoon salt
¼ teaspoon dry mustard
   Dash pepper

In a pie plate, toast the almonds at 400° for 10 minutes. In a skillet, cook bacon until crisp; crumble. Tear lettuce. Combine almonds, bacon, lettuce, oranges and mushrooms.

To prepare dressing, combine oil, vinegar, cheese, salt, dry mustard and pepper in a jar; shake to blend. Pour dressing over all.

Serves 4.

STUFFED MUSHROOMS

36 medium mushrooms (about 1 pound)
5 tablespoons butter
   Salt and pepper
¼ pound shallots, minced
1½ teaspoons flour
½ cup heavy cream
3 tablespoons minced parsley
   Salt and pepper to taste
¼ cup grated Swiss cheese

Wash and dry mushrooms; remove stems. Mince stems and reserve. Melt 3 tablespoons of the butter in a 15 x 10½ x 1-inch jelly roll pan and arrange mushroom caps in the pan, hollow sides up. Season lightly with salt and pepper.

In a skillet, melt remaining butter and sauté mushroom stems and shallots 4 to 5 minutes. Lower heat, stir in flour and cook 1 minute. Add cream, parsley and seasonings, stirring until thickened. Fill caps with mixture and top each with grated cheese. Bake at 350° for 10 minutes.(*)

3 dozen.

(*)May be prepared in advance. Refrigerate up to 24 hours or freeze, covered with foil. If frozen, bake unthawed, covered, at 350° for 15 minutes. Remove foil and broil 3 to 5 minutes to brown tops. If refrigerated, bring to room temperature and broil 3 to 5 minutes.

OLIVE-STUFFED MUSHROOMS

24 medium mushrooms
 1 teaspoon salt
 2 tablespoons butter
 2 tablespoons vegetable oil
 1 medium onion, minced
 2 cloves garlic, minced
   Dash thyme
   Dash pepper
 ½ cup pitted black olives, finely chopped
 3 egg yolks, beaten
 ¼ cup freshly grated Parmesan cheese

Wash and dry mushrooms; remove stems. Chop stems and reserve. Place mushroom caps, hollow sides up, in a large skillet. Sprinkle with salt. Heat 1 tablespoon of the butter and 1 tablespoon of the oil and sprinkle over caps. Cover and cook over low heat for 10 minutes. Remove mushrooms from skillet and place, hollow sides up, on a cookie sheet. Refrigerate until cool.

Heat remaining butter and oil and sauté chopped mushroom stems 3 minutes. Add onion, garlic, thyme, pepper and olives. Cover and simmer 12 minutes longer. Cool slightly, then gradually stir in egg yolks. Cook, stirring 1 minute; cool. Stuff caps with mixture and sprinkle with grated cheese.(*) Bake at 375° for 25 to 30 minutes.

2 dozen.

(*)May be prepared in advance to this point. Refrigerate up to 48 hours. To serve, bring to room temperature and bake as directed above.

MUSHROOMS PARMESAN

2 tablespoons butter
2 cups sliced fresh mushrooms
2 teaspoons lemon juice
¼ cup grated Parmesan cheese
2 tablespoons minced onion
2 eggs, slightly beaten
1 cup milk
1 tablespoon flour
  Salt and pepper to taste
¼ cup dry bread crumbs

In a skillet, melt butter and sauté mushrooms 5 minutes; add lemon juice. Place in a buttered 8 x 8 x 2-inch baking dish and sprinkle with cheese and onion. Combine eggs, milk, flour, salt and pepper and beat well. Pour over mushrooms. Sprinkle top with bread crumbs.(*) Bake at 375° for 20 minutes.

Serves 4.

(*)May be prepared in advance to this point. Refrigerate up to 24 hours. To serve, bring to room temperature and bake as directed above.

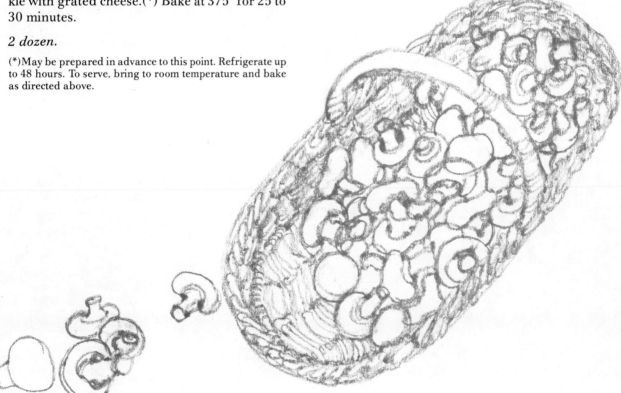

ONIONS

ONION SOUP

    1 loaf French bread
      Butter
    4 medium onions
 ¼ cup butter
    5 tablespoons tomato paste
    1 cup grated Swiss cheese

Cut French bread into ½-inch-thick slices; toast and butter them.

Cut onions into very thin slices. Melt ¼ cup butter and sauté onions until limp. In a flame-proof 2-quart casserole, alternate layers of bread slices, onions, tomato paste and cheese, using about ⅓ at a time. Repeat layers to fill casserole ⅔ full. Place a metal or glass funnel through to bottom of casserole, at one edge, and slowly pour in hot salted water until top layer of bread is swimming.

Place casserole on top of stove and simmer, uncovered, 30 minutes. Add more hot salted water as needed.

Place casserole in 350° oven and bake 1 hour, adding hot salted water through funnel as needed.

The soup is ready when the surface is baked and looks like a crusty golden cake; the ingredients should be thick and well blended with a little liquid. Each person's serving should be topped with some of the crust.

Serves 4 as a main dish.

GREEN ONION PIE

      9-inch Pie Shell (below)
 ¼ cup butter
    3 cups thinly sliced green onions with tops
    1 teaspoon salt
 ⅛ teaspoon pepper
      Dash cayenne pepper
 ½ teaspoon caraway seeds
    1 cup milk
    1 cup sour cream
    2 eggs, lightly beaten

Prepare Pie Shell. In a large skillet, melt butter and sauté green onions 5 minutes. Season with salt, pepper, cayenne and caraway seeds. Blend in the remaining ingredients. Pour into pie shell.(*) Bake at 400° for 15 minutes. Reduce heat to 350° and bake until set, 30 to 40 minutes longer.

Serves 8.

Pie Shell

    1 cup flour
 ½ teaspoon salt
 ½ teaspoon sugar
 ½ cup butter
    2 tablespoons milk

Combine flour, salt and sugar; cut in butter until crumbly. Stir in milk. Chill until dough is easy to handle. Roll out for 9-inch pie plate. Flute edges and prick all over.

(*)May be prepared in advance to this point. Refrigerate up to 24 hours or freeze. To serve, bring to room temperature and bake as directed above.

BAKED ONIONS

 1½ pounds small white onions
 ¼ cup butter
 ¼ cup light brown sugar
    1 cup crushed cornflakes
      Whole cloves

Peel whole onions and parboil 15 minutes. In a saucepan, cook and stir butter and brown sugar together until bubbly. Roll onions in butter mixture, then in crushed cornflakes. Reserve remaining butter mixture. Stick a whole clove in each onion. Place in a 13½ x 9 x 2-inch baking dish and pour remaining butter sauce over all.(*) Bake at 350° for 20 to 30 minutes.

Serves 4.

(*)May be prepared in advance to this point. Refrigerate up to 24 hours. To serve, bring to room temperature and bake as directed above.

PARSLEY

GLORIA'S
APPETIZER PROVENÇAL

- 3 cloves garlic
- 1½ teaspoons salt
- ¼ teaspoon dried hot red pepper
- 1 onion, minced
- 1 large carrot, grated
- 1½ cups snipped Italian parsley
- ¼ cup wine vinegar
- ¼ cup vegetable oil
- ¼ cup olive oil
- 1 can (2 ounces) flat anchovies,
  cut into 1-inch pieces

At least 4 days in advance of serving, place garlic and salt in a wooden bowl. Using the back of a spoon, rub them together until pulpy. Add dried pepper and crush into garlic. Add onion, carrot, parsley, vinegar and oils; mix well.

In a glass bowl, alternate layers of anchovies and parsley sauce, ending with sauce; refrigerate (may be refrigerated up to 1 week). To serve, let guests help themselves, mounding mixture on bite-size pieces of Italian bread.

About 2½ cups.

PESTO

- 4 cups fresh basil leaves, firmly packed
- 1 cup fresh Italian parsley, stems removed
- ¼ pound Parmesan cheese, freshly grated
- ½ cup pine nuts
- ¼ cup walnuts
- 1 clove garlic
- 1 teaspoon salt
- 1 tablespoon butter
- ¾ cup olive oil
- 2 pounds hot cooked spaghetti

This recipe originated in Genoa, where housewives gather fresh young basil leaves and pound them with mortar and pestle into a paste. Until recently, I had modernized the recipe for my own use by combining small amounts of the ingredients at a time and blending them in the blender. I now own a food processor and find that it is the speediest method for making Pesto.

The point is to combine all the above ingredients into a smooth green paste with whatever appliance you have. It's difficult to be exact about the amount of oil, but start with ½ cup and keep adding until the mixture is the consistency of mayonnaise.(*)

Toss sauce with hot spaghetti (the sauce is never cooked) and admire the unusual color.

Serves 8 as a main dish.

(*)May be refrigerated up to 3 days or frozen.

PEAS

It takes about 2 pounds of fresh peas or about 2 cupfuls of shelled peas to serve four. If you grow them in your garden, you know better than most that it takes a lot of peas and a lot of shelling to serve just a few people. Therefore, I'm more apt to use frozen peas, especially the tiny ones — but I rarely use canned peas.

Fresh peas should be cooked in 2 scant tablespoons of butter and a dash of salt — and sometimes covered with a moist lettuce leaf. Water can, of course, be used instead of butter (about 1 inch), but I prefer the butter. Cook, covered, until tender, about 10 minutes.

I like to serve peas with chopped parsley and a dash of white pepper or a bit of chopped fresh mint. Tarragon is also a nice touch.

Snow peas, also called Chinese pea pods, are edible without shelling. They're very easy to grow and need only to have the tip and "string" removed before cooking. Snow peas are also available frozen, but, to me, they seem to lose all their crispness in the freezing process and are not nearly as good. Snow peas require only the slightest amount of cooking time — 2 minutes at most.

PARSNIPS

DACIE'S
PARSNIP CIRCLES

  2 **pounds parsnips**
½ **cup butter**
     Salt and pepper to taste

Scrub parsnips and parboil whole in salted water until crisp-tender, 15 to 20 mintues; chill. Peel and slice into ½-inch circles. Fry parsnips in butter 15 to 20 minutes, turning often to brown evenly. At end of cooking time, turn up heat for a few moments until parsnips become crisp on outside. Season.

Parsnips may also be parboiled as above, chilled, peeled and placed with a roast of beef or leg of lamb while it roasts.

Serves 4.

VEGETARIAN
CHOPPED LIVER

  3 **onions, diced**
  2 **tablespoons vegetable oil**
  3 **hard-boiled eggs**
  1 **can (8½ ounces) peas, drained**
     Salt and pepper
  1 **can (8½ ounces) French-cut green beans, drained**
  1 **cup walnuts**
  2 **tablespoons dry bread crumbs**

Combine all ingredients except bread crumbs and put through a meat grinder or food processor. Clean out grinder with the bread crumbs. If using a food processor, add bread crumbs to vegetable-nut mixture. Mix well and add additional salt and pepper, if necessary; chill (may be refrigerated up to 48 hours).

Serve this on party rye bread — and, believe it or not, it tastes like chopped liver.

About 1½ cups.

PEAS WITH DILL

  1 cup sour cream
  ¼ cup mayonnaise
  ¼ cup chopped green onions
  ¼ cup chopped fresh dill
  3 cups green peas, cooked and cooled
    Salt and pepper to taste

To prepare dressing, combine sour cream, mayonnaise, green onions and dill. Toss peas in dressing and season with salt and pepper; chill well before serving (may be refrigerated up to 48 hours).

Serves 6.

PEAS AND CAULIFLOWER PARMESAN

    Moist lettuce leaves
  2 pounds fresh peas, shelled
  1 teaspoon sugar
  2 to 4 tablespoons water
  ½ teaspoon salt
  1 head (about 2½ pounds) cauliflower
  3 tablespoons butter, melted
  ½ cup grated Parmesan cheese

Line the bottom of a heavy saucepan with lettuce leaves. Place peas on lettuce and add sugar, water and salt. Cover and cook over low heat 15 to 20 minutes.

Break cauliflower into small flowerets. Cover and cook in boiling salted water until tender, 8 to 10 minutes; drain. Combine peas and cauliflower. Pour melted butter over all and sprinkle with grated Parmesan cheese.

Serves 8.

MINTED NEW PEAS

  2 pounds fresh peas, shelled, or 1 package
    (10 ounces) frozen peas
  1 teaspoon dried mint
  1 tablespoon butter
  1 tablespoon crème de menthe

Cover and cook peas in lightly salted boiling water with dried mint until just tender, about 10 minutes. (Cook frozen peas according to package directions, adding dried mint.) Drain and add butter and crème de menthe.

Serves 4.

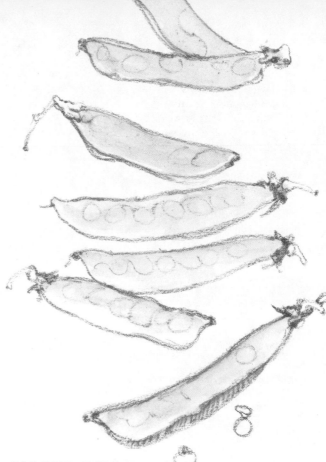

SNOW PEAS AND MUSHROOMS

  ½ pound fresh snow peas
  ¾ cup chicken broth
  1 tablespoon cornstarch
  ¼ cup oyster sauce (buy in Chinese grocery)
  1 teaspoon sugar
  1 tablespoon soy sauce
  6 tablespoons peanut oil
  ¼ cup thinly sliced canned bamboo shoots
  1 can (10 ounces) abalone mushrooms, drained
    and cubed (buy in Chinese grocery)
  1 can (10 ounces) golden mushrooms, drained
    (buy in Chinese grocery)

String snow peas and cut in half diagonally. Blend chicken broth and cornstarch. Mix oyster sauce, sugar and soy sauce.

In a wok or large skillet, heat 2 tablespoons of the oil and stir-fry snow peas and bamboo shoots together for 30 seconds; remove from pan. Add 2 more tablespoons of the oil and stir-fry mushrooms 45 seconds; remove from pan.

Add remaining oil and heat oyster sauce mixture. Add cornstarch paste. When sauce boils and thickens, return vegetables to pan, stir and serve immediately.

Serves 4.

CHINESE VEGETABLES

  6 large mushrooms
  2 tablespoons peanut oil
  ½ cup thinly sliced canned bamboo shoots
  2 packages (6 ounces each) frozen snow peas, thawed
  ½ teaspoon sugar
  1½ teaspoons salt
  ¼ cup chicken broth

Wash, dry and slice mushrooms. In a wok or large skillet, heat oil and stir-fry mushrooms and bamboo shoots 2 minutes. Add snow peas, sugar, salt and broth. Stir-fry over high heat 2 minutes longer. Serve immediately.

Serves 6.

CHINESE SNOW PEAS

  ½ cup canned bamboo shoots
  6 dried Chinese mushrooms (buy in Chinese grocery)
  1 pound fresh snow peas
  2 tablespoons peanut oil
  1½ teaspoons salt
  ½ teaspoon sugar

Slice bamboo shoots and cut them into triangles; reserve. Soak mushrooms in warm water 20 minutes. Reserve water and dice mushrooms, discarding tough stems. String snow peas.

In a wok or large skillet, heat oil and stir-fry mushrooms and bamboo shoots 2 minutes. Add snow peas, salt, sugar and 2 tablespoons of the reserved mushroom water. Cook 2 minutes. Serve immediately.

Serves 4.

PEPPERS

SHIRLEY'S STUFFED PEPPERS

  1 jar (32 ounces) cherry peppers
  1 can (7 ounces) tuna, drained and mashed
  2 cans (2 ounces each) anchovy fillets, cut up
  1 can (7½ ounces) pitted black olives, drained and minced
  1 stalk celery, minced
    Olive oil

Drain peppers, reserving brine. Mix tuna with anchovies, olives and celery. Remove stems and seeds from cherry peppers and stuff cavities with tuna mixture. Place peppers in a 1-quart jar and return reserved brine. Put layer of olive oil on top of brine; cover. Let stand at least overnight before serving. Will keep for weeks!

1 quart.

SHRIMP-STUFFED PEPPERS

  2 large red bell peppers
  3 tablespoons butter
  ¼ cup finely chopped onion
  ¼ cup flour
  1 cup sour cream
  1 teaspoon lemon juice
  1 teaspoon Dijon-type mustard
  2 tablespoons chopped parsley
  2 cups (about ¾ pound) cooked shrimp
  1 can (8 ounces) water chestnuts, sliced
    Salt and pepper to taste
  ½ cup shredded Monterey Jack cheese

Cut peppers in half lengthwise; remove seeds. Drop into boiling water, cover and cook 4 minutes; drain.

Melt butter and sauté onion until golden. Stir in flour, then blend in sour cream. Add lemon juice, mustard, parsley, shrimp, water chestnuts and salt and pepper. Spoon into pepper shells. Sprinkle cheese over top.(*) Place in an 8 x 8 x 2-inch baking pan and broil 6 inches from heat 3 to 5 minutes.

Serves 4 as a main dish.

(*)May be prepared in advance to this point. Refrigerate up to 24 hours. To serve, heat at 350° for 20 minutes, then run under broiler to brown cheese.

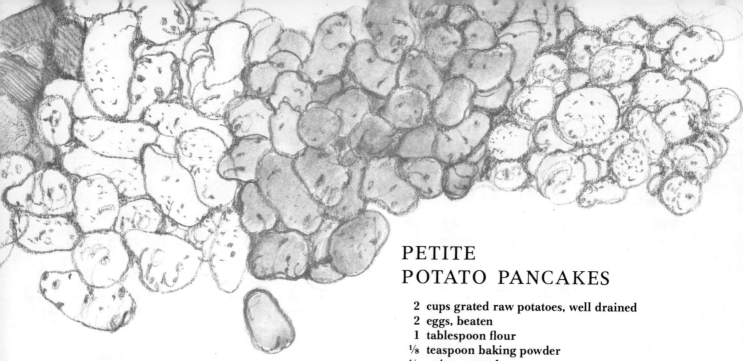

POTATOES

Potatoes should be scrubbed, any sprouts removed and either boiled, covered, in salted water until tender or baked in a preheated 400° oven for about 1 hour. Serve dressed with butter, salt and pepper. For a change, add chopped parsley or chives and sour cream. For both flavor and nutrition, potatoes should be cooked in their skins. And, of course, your family will always welcome potatoes that have been sautéed in oil or deep-fried.

Sweet potatoes, though botanically not in the same family, are certainly similar in that they are starchy and can be readily boiled or baked. They are particularly good when baked, the insides removed, mashed and mixed with butter and crushed pineapple and stuffed back into the shells.

Contrary to popular belief, potatoes themselves are not fattening and contain no more calories than most apples and oranges. So, if you are dieting, don't discard the potato — just discard the trimmings.

Most American families don't consider a dinner (or even a lunch) complete without potatoes. And they arrive day after day, baked, boiled or fried, and there's nothing wrong with that. However, potatoes do deserve more than the casual attention they seem to get. Following you will find a wealth of potato dishes that I think will earn greater respect for the "old standby."

PETITE POTATO PANCAKES

    2 cups grated raw potatoes, well drained
    2 eggs, beaten
    1 tablespoon flour
    ⅛ teaspoon baking powder
    ½ onion, grated
    1½ teaspoons salt
       Dash pepper
       Applesauce for dipping

Combine all ingredients except applesauce and mix thoroughly. Drop by tablespoonfuls into a well-greased skillet and brown on both sides. Drain on paper towels.(*) Serve with applesauce as a dip. A terrific hors d'oeuvre!

About 30.

(*)May be refrigerated up to 24 hours or frozen. To serve, bring to room temperature and reheat at 450° until very crisp.

RED POTATO SALAD

    2 pounds small red new potatoes
    2 stalks celery, diced
    3 hard-boiled eggs, quartered
    1 cup sour cream
    2 tablespoons vinegar
    2 teaspoons prepared horseradish
    1 teaspoon sugar
    1 tablespoon fresh dill (1½ teaspoons dried)
    ¼ teaspoon dry mustard
    ½ teaspoon salt
       Freshly ground black pepper

Scrub unpeeled potatoes. Cover and boil in salted water 20 minutes. Drain and rinse in cold water; peel while still warm. Slice potatoes into a bowl with celery and eggs.

To prepare dressing, mix remaining ingredients and toss with potatoes until all are coated. Chill before serving (may be refrigerated up to 48 hours).

Serves 8.

IDAHO FRITTERS

    2 Idaho potatoes
    2 egg yolks
    1 cup cold water
 1¼ cups flour
    1 teaspoon salt
    1 teaspoon paprika
    2 teaspoons curry powder
      Oil or shortening in deep-fat fryer

Scrub, peel and thinly slice potatoes. Spread on paper towels to dry. Mix remaining ingredients lightly — batter should be a little lumpy. Dip potatoes in batter and deep-fry until fritters are puffy and golden. Serve immediately.

Serves 4.

SWEDISH ROAST POTATOES

    6 medium potatoes
  ¼ cup butter, melted
    1 teaspoon salt
      Dash pepper
  ½ teaspoon paprika
  ¼ cup grated Cheddar cheese

Scrub and peel potatoes. Slash them partway through, leaving bottoms intact. Roll potatoes in melted butter. Place in a roasting pan around meat about 2 hours before meat is done. Sprinkle with salt, pepper and paprika. Baste frequently with pan drippings. After 1 hour and 30 minutes, sprinkle with grated cheese.

Serves 6.

CRUSTY POTATO BALLS

 12 new potatoes
    2 tablespoons butter, melted
      Seasoned salt and pepper to taste
  ½ cup crushed branflakes

Scrub potatoes and parboil 8 minutes; peel. Roll potatoes in melted butter with seasoned salt and pepper, then in crushed branflakes.(*) Bake on a foil-covered cookie sheet at 400° for 25 minutes.

Serves 4.

(*)May be prepared in advance to this point. Refrigerate up to 24 hours. To serve, bring to room temperature and bake as directed above.

POTATO SCONES

 2½ tablespoons butter
    2 cups self-rising flour
      Salt
 1½ cups mashed cooked potatoes
  ¼ cup milk
      Caraway seeds

Cut butter into flour and add a good pinch of salt. Mix in mashed potatoes and pour in milk to make a soft dough. Roll out dough on floured board and cut into rounds about 3 inches in diameter. Sprinkle with caraway seeds and dot with additional butter. Bake on a greased cookie sheet at 450° for 20 minutes.(*)

12 scones.

(*)May be refrigerated up to 24 hours. To serve, bring to room temperature and reheat at 450° about 10 minutes, until heated through.

POTATO SOUFFLE GRUYERE

    4 cups mashed cooked potatoes (about 6)
    ¼ cup soft butter
    2 ounces Gruyère cheese, grated
    2 tablespoons minced chives
    1 teaspoon salt
    ⅛ teaspoon pepper
    3 eggs, separated
    1 cup heavy cream, whipped

Combine mashed potatoes, butter, cheese, chives, salt and pepper. Beat egg yolks and fold into whipped cream, then fold into potato mixture. Beat egg whites until stiff and fold into potato mixture. Spoon into a greased 6-cup soufflé dish. Bake at 350° for 1 hour. Serve soufflé immediately.

Serves 8.

IRISH SCALLOPED POTATO CASSEROLE

    2 cups grated Swiss cheese
    ½ cup sliced green onions, with tops
    1 tablespoon dill weed
    2 tablespoons butter
    2 tablespoons flour
    1 teaspoon salt
    1 cup milk
    1 cup sour cream
    6 to 7 cups sliced cooked potatoes (4 large)
    3 cups diced cooked ham (about 1 pound)

In a small bowl, toss 1 cup of the Swiss cheese, the green onions and dill; reserve.

In a 1-quart saucepan, melt butter and stir in flour and salt. Gradually add milk, stirring until thickened. Cook 2 minutes longer. Remove from heat and stir in sour cream; reserve.

In a 3-quart casserole, layer ⅓ of the potatoes, half the ham, half the reserved cheese mixture and half the sour cream mixture. Repeat, ending with last ⅓ of the potatoes. Top with remaining Swiss cheese.(*) Bake at 350° for 30 minutes.

Serves 6 as a main dish.

(*)May be prepared in advance to this point. Refrigerate up to 24 hours. To serve, bring to room temperature and bake as directed above.

ORANGE-GLAZED SWEETS

    6 sweet potatoes, cooked, peeled and sliced
    1 orange, thinly sliced, with rind
    ⅓ cup light brown sugar
    ⅓ cup granulated sugar
    1 tablespoon cornstarch
    1 cup orange juice
    2 teaspoons grated orange rind
      Pinch salt

Arrange sweet potatoes and orange slices in a buttered 13 x 9 x 2-inch baking dish. Combine sugars and cornstarch; stir in orange juice, rind and salt. Pour sauce over sweet potatoes.(*) Cover baking dish with aluminum foil and bake at 350° for 30 minutes. Remove foil and bake 30 minutes longer.

Serves 6.

(*)May be prepared in advance to this point. Refrigerate up to 24 hours. To serve, bring to room temperature and bake as directed above.

SWEET POTATO SURPRISE BALLS

    4 large cooked sweet potatoes
    1 egg
    2 tablespoons orange juice
    3 tablespoons butter
    ¼ teaspoon vanilla
    6 marshmallows
    ¼ cup cornflake crumbs

Mash sweet potatoes. Mix in egg, orange juice, 1 tablespoon of the butter and the vanilla. Beat together until fluffy. Form mixture into 6 balls with a marshmallow in the center of each. Roll in cornflake crumbs.(*)

Melt remaining butter and pour over balls in a baking dish. Bake at 400° for 10 minutes.

Serves 6.

(*)May be prepared in advance to this point. Refrigerate up to 24 hours. To serve, bring to room temperature and bake as directed above.

HONEY PUMPKIN PIE

- 2 cups canned pumpkin
- 1 cup evaporated milk
- ¾ cup honey
- ¼ cup cognac
- 1 tablespoon finely chopped crystallized ginger
- 1 teaspoon cinnamon
- ¼ teaspoon ground allspice
- ½ teaspoon salt
- 3 eggs, beaten
  Unbaked 9-inch pie shell

Combine all ingredients except pie shell; mix well. Pour into pie shell.(*) Bake at 425° for 15 minutes; reduce heat to 350° and bake 45 minutes longer or until knife inserted in custard comes out clean.

Serves 8.

(*)May be prepared in advance to this point. Refrigerate up to 24 hours or freeze. To serve, bring to room temperature and bake as directed above.

PUMPKIN CRUNCH PIE

- 22 vanilla wafers or gingersnaps
- 1 pint vanilla ice cream, softened
- 1 can (16 ounces) pumpkin
- 1 cup sugar
- ½ teaspoon salt
- 1 teaspoon cinnamon
- ½ teaspoon ground ginger
- ¼ teaspoon ground cloves
- 1 teaspoon vanilla
- 1 cup heavy cream
- 1 cup slivered blanched almonds
- ¼ cup sugar
- ½ cup heavy cream

Line a 10-inch pie plate with wafers; spread with ice cream. Freeze until firm.

Combine pumpkin, 1 cup sugar, the salt, cinnamon, ginger, cloves and vanilla. Whip 1 cup heavy cream and fold into pumpkin mixture. Pour over ice cream. Cover with aluminum foil and freeze until firm, at least 4 hours.

In a small skillet, combine almonds and ¼ cup sugar. Cook over low heat, stirring constantly, until almonds become caramel colored. Remove from heat and spread on waxed paper. When cool, break almonds apart; reserve. Fifteen minutes before serving, remove pie from freezer. Whip ½ cup heavy cream; garnish pie with whipped cream and reserved almonds.

Serves 8.

PUMPKIN

PUMPKIN BREAD

- 4 cups sifted flour
- 2 teaspoons baking soda
- 1 teaspoon baking powder
- 1½ teaspoons salt
- 2½ cups sugar
- 1 teaspoon nutmeg
- 1 teaspoon allspice
- 1 teaspoon cinnamon
- ½ teaspoon ground cloves
- 1 cup vegetable oil
- ⅔ cup cold water
- 4 eggs
- 1 can (16 ounces) pumpkin
- ½ cup chopped walnuts

Combine flour, baking soda, baking powder, salt and sugar. Add spices. Mix in oil and water. Beat in eggs, one at a time, and add pumpkin and walnuts.

Pour into a 12 x 4½ x 2¾-inch loaf pan and bake at 350° for 55 to 60 minutes. If you wish to use 2 smaller pans, bake 40 to 50 minutes.(*)

1 loaf.

(*)May be refrigerated up to 48 hours or frozen. To serve, bring to room temperature.

RHUBARB

Rhubarb, like the pumpkin and avocado, is a "fruity" vegetable. Although many people think of them as fruits, botanically all three are classified as vegetables. Rhubarb is one of my favorites. When it is in season, early in the spring, I freeze as much as I can for use all year long. It freezes beautifully.

I wash the stalks and discard the leaves, then cut the rhubarb into 1-inch pieces. I place the rhubarb in a saucepan with about half as much sugar as there is fruit. For a special treat, I sometimes cut a pineapple into pieces of the same size and add them to the saucepan. Let the fruit sit with the sugar for 30 minutes, then cover the pan and place over very low heat. As the sugar melts, it draws the juices from the fruit and makes enough liquid to cook the fruit. When the fruit is tender, turn off the heat and, if desired, toss with a basketful of strawberries, washed and hulled. Cover the pan and the berries will cook in the accumulated steam and remain whole and semi-firm.

Cooked rhubarb, either mixed with other fruits or not, may be refrigerated up to 72 hours or frozen.

RHUBARB CRUNCH

- 1 cup quick-cooking rolled oats
- ½ cup flour
- ¾ cup light brown sugar
- ½ cup butter
- 1 cup granulated sugar
- ½ cup water
- 4 cups cut rhubarb (1-inch lengths)

Mix rolled oats, flour and brown sugar; cut in butter until crumbly. Pat half the mixture onto bottom of a greased 8 x 8 x 2-inch baking pan. Reserve remaining mixture.

In a saucepan, combine granulated sugar and water; bring to a boil. Add rhubarb; reduce heat, cover and simmer 10 minutes. Drain rhubarb, reserving syrup. Puree rhubarb in blender or food processor. Spread over oatmeal mixture in baking pan. Top with reserved oatmeal mixture. Bake at 350° for 45 minutes.(*) Serve warm with reserved syrup.

Serves 8.

(*)May be prepared in advance to this point. Refrigerate up to 24 hours. Reheat and serve as directed above.

RHUBARB CREAM

- 1½ pounds rhubarb, cut into 1-inch lengths
- ½ cup apple juice
- ¾ cup light brown sugar
- ½ teaspoon cinnamon
- 3 eggs, separated
- 1 cup heavy cream, whipped

In a saucepan, combine rhubarb and apple juice and bring to a boil; reduce heat, cover and simmer until tender, about 10 minutes. Blend until smooth in a blender or food processor. Return to saucepan and beat in brown sugar, cinnamon and egg yolks. Heat, stirring, until mixture thickens—do not boil! Cool and chill.

Beat egg whites until stiff and fold into chilled rhubarb mixture, then fold in whipped cream. Chill before serving (may be refrigerated up to 24 hours).

Serves 6.

SPINACH BALLS

2 packages (10 ounces each) frozen chopped
   spinach
1½ cups herb stuffing mix
1 cup grated Parmesan cheese
3 eggs, beaten
¾ cup soft butter

Cook spinach according to package directions; drain. Combine all ingredients and roll into bite-size balls; freeze.

To serve, place on a foil-covered cookie sheet and bake unthawed in a preheated oven at 350° for 15 minutes.

About 3 dozen hors d'oeuvres.

SUSAN'S SPINACH SALAD

¾ cup vegetable oil
1 tablespoon olive oil
2 tablespoons wine vinegar
1 tablespoon sugar
¼ cup chopped parsley
1 tablespoon chopped chives
2 shallots
1 small onion, chopped
½ cup mayonnaise
1½ pounds spinach, washed, dried and
   chopped
2 hard-boiled egg yolks, chopped
6 slices crisp cooked bacon, crumbled
½ pound fresh mushrooms, sliced
½ cup grated Parmesan cheese

To prepare dressing, combine oils, vinegar, sugar, parsley, chives, shallots, onion and mayonnaise in a blender or food processor. Blend until smooth (may be refrigerated up to 24 hours).

Toss spinach, egg yolks, bacon, mushrooms and cheese. Pour dressing over all and toss again. If desired, garnish with additional chopped chives. Serve as a first course, salad or main dish.

Serves 6 to 8.

SPINACH

As with so many vegetables, the best method of cooking spinach is probably the simplest. First and foremost, wash the spinach — no matter what the package may say. Wash it quickly in several pots of cold water, rinsing and draining each time. This will get rid of any sand or grit. Also, you ought to remove the tough ribs of the larger leaves. Next, place the rinsed leaves in a large pot (the moisture that clings to the leaves provides all the water you'll need) and add salt to taste; cover and cook until just tender — young spinach should take about 6 minutes, older spinach a bit longer. Two pounds of fresh spinach will cook down to the amount needed for four.

Add butter, lemon juice or more salt and pepper as you wish. I like to add a touch of nutmeg. For a nice change, try olive oil and garlic instead of butter. If you like creamed vegetables, spinach will be a favorite and, of course, raw spinach is super in salads. In many recipes, frozen spinach is not too bad a substitute when you don't want to bother with fresh.

SPINACH-SPROUT SALAD

- 1 pound fresh spinach leaves, washed and drained
- ¾ pound fresh bean sprouts
- 6 tablespoons salad oil
- 3 tablespoons cider vinegar
- 3 tablespoons chili sauce
- ½ teaspoon salt
  Dash pepper
- 2 hard-boiled eggs, quartered

Tear spinach and combine with bean sprouts.

To prepare dressing, mix oil, vinegar, chili sauce, salt and pepper. Toss dressing with spinach and sprouts and garnish with egg quarters.

Serves 6.

BAKED HERBED SPINACH

- 2 tablespoons butter
- ½ cup finely chopped onion
- 1 clove garlic, minced
- 2 packages (10 ounces each) frozen spinach, thawed
- ½ cup heavy cream
- ½ cup milk
- ¼ cup grated Parmesan cheese
- ¼ cup dry bread crumbs
- ½ teaspoon marjoram
- ½ teaspoon salt
- ⅛ teaspoon pepper
- 2 tablespoons grated Parmesan cheese

Melt butter and sauté onion and garlic until limp. In a greased 1-quart casserole, combine all ingredients except 2 tablespoons cheese. Sprinkle remaining cheese on top.(*) Bake, uncovered, at 350° until cheese is brown, about 45 minutes.

Serves 4 or 5.

(*)May be prepared in advance to this point. Refrigerate up to 24 hours. To serve, bring to room temperature and bake as directed above.

CHILE SPINACH

- 3 eggs
- 3 tablespoons flour
- 3 packages (10 ounces each) frozen chopped spinach, thawed
- 2 cups cottage cheese
- 2 cups grated Cheddar cheese
- 1 can (3 ounces) green chilies, chopped
  Salt and pepper to taste

Beat eggs and flour until smooth. Combine all ingredients and pour into a greased 2-quart casserole.(*) Bake, uncovered, at 350° for 1 hour. Let stand a few minutes before serving.

Serves 8.

(*)May be prepared in advance to this point. Refrigerate up to 24 hours. To serve, bring to room temperature and bake as directed above.

GREEN AND WHITE PIE

- Unbaked 9-inch pie shell
- 1 tablespoon butter
- 1 cup minced onion
- 1 package (10 ounces) frozen chopped spinach, thawed
- 15 ounces ricotta cheese
- 2 eggs
- ¾ teaspoon salt
- ⅛ teaspoon pepper
- ⅛ teaspoon nutmeg
- ¼ cup freshly grated Parmesan cheese

Heat oven to 400°. Prick pie shell all over. Bake 10 minutes.

Melt butter and sauté onion until soft. Add well-drained spinach and toss until all liquid is absorbed.

In bowl, combine remaining ingredients and mix well. Add spinach-onion mixture and mix until it looks like marble. Pour mixture into pie shell.

Reduce heat to 350° and bake 40 to 45 minutes or until top is golden. Cool 10 minutes before slicing.

Serves 6 as a main dish.

SPINACH-FILLED CREPES

    Crepes (below)
2 packages (10 ounces each) frozen chopped
      spinach
¼ cup butter
2 tablespoons minced shallots
¼ cup flour
1 cup milk
1 cup chicken broth
    Salt and pepper to taste
    Dash nutmeg
1 can (4 ounces) chopped mushrooms, drained
½ cup grated Swiss cheese

Prepare Crepes. Cook spinach according to package directions; drain.

In a large skillet, melt butter and brown shallots. Stir in flour. Remove from heat and gradually stir in milk and broth. Return to low heat, stirring until thickened. Season with salt, pepper and nutmeg. Combine spinach and mushrooms with half the sauce. Divide filling among crepes, placing it toward a lower edge, then roll up. Place in a 13 x 9 x 2-inch baking dish. Add grated cheese to remaining sauce and use sauce to top crepes.(*) Bake at 375° for 30 minutes or until brown and bubbly.

12 crepes.

Crepes

¼ cup flour
1 egg
1 egg yolk
1 cup milk
1 tablespoon vegetable oil

In a small bowl, combine flour, egg, egg yolk, 3 tablespoons of the milk and the oil. Beat until smooth. Stir in remaining milk. Refrigerate at least 3 hours (may be refrigerated up to 1 week).

Heat a 6-inch crepe pan and wipe with buttered waxed paper. Lower heat. For each crepe, cover bottom of the pan with batter. Cook until golden on one side, turn and cook until golden on second side.

(*)Filled crepes may be prepared in advance to this point. Refrigerate up to 24 hours or freeze. To serve, bring to room temperature and bake as directed above.

SPINACH SAUCE WITH FETTUCINI

½ cup olive oil
2 packages (10 ounces each) frozen chopped
      spinach, thawed
3 cloves garlic, minced
1 cup chicken broth
1 can (2 ounces) anchovy fillets, mashed
1 tablespoon chopped fresh basil
½ cup chopped fresh parsley
1 cup grated Parmesan cheese
1½ cups ricotta cheese
    Salt and pepper to taste
2 pounds uncooked fettucini
¼ cup butter, melted
2 eggs, beaten
    Pepper to taste

In a large skillet, heat half the oil; add spinach, garlic and half the broth. Cook, stirring, 5 minutes. Combine remaining oil and broth, the anchovies, basil, parsley and cheeses. Beat until smooth. Fold in spinach and season with salt and pepper.(*)

Meanwhile, cook fettucini until al dente; drain. Toss hot fettucini with melted butter, eggs and pepper. Pour spinach sauce over hot fettucini. Toss and serve immediately.

Serves 8 as a main dish.

(*)May be prepared in advance to this point. Refrigerate up to 24 hours or freeze. To serve, bring to room temperature and proceed as directed above.

SQUASH

Squash, of one variety or another, is readily available all year long. Perhaps the most common of the summer squashes are the yellow crooknecks and the green zucchini. In most recipes they are interchangeable. Most simply taken, they are washed, the bud and stem ends removed and the squash cut into 1-inch slices. Drop the sliced squash into boiling salted water to which you can add a chicken bouillon cube and/or some minced onion. Cover and simmer until just tender, about 10 to 15 minutes. Drain well. Serve with butter, salt and pepper or any number of seasonings such as tarragon, basil, chives or nutmeg.

Of the winter squashes, butternut and acorn come to mind first. I like them simply baked, peeled, seeded and served with butter. Acorn squash halves may be filled with butter and brown sugar, or a combination of applesauce, chopped nuts and raisins. Crushed pineapple makes a good filler, too.

MARGARET'S COLD SQUASH SOUP

- 2 to 3 pounds yellow summer squash
- 2 medium onions, chopped
- 3 cups chicken broth
  Salt, pepper, nutmeg and dill to taste
- 1 cup sour cream
  Chopped chives

Wash and cut up squash. Add to saucepan with onions, 2 cups of the broth and the seasonings. Cover and simmer 30 minutes; cool. Puree in a blender or food processor. Add remaining broth, stir in sour cream and chill until ready to serve (may be refrigerated up to 48 hours). Garnish with chives.

Serves 8.

ARABIAN SQUASH

- 1 pound yellow summer squash, grated
- ¼ teaspoon salt
- ½ cup grated Cheddar cheese
- ⅓ cup cottage cheese
- 2 eggs
- ⅓ cup dry bread crumbs
- 1 tablespoon minced parsley
  Pepper to taste
- 2 tablespoons butter, melted
- ½ clove garlic, crushed
- 2 tablespoons grated Parmesan cheese

Squeeze water out of squash. Combine all ingredients except Parmesan cheese and place in a 1-quart casserole.(*) Top with cheese and bake, uncovered, at 350° for 1 hour.

Serves 4.

(*)May be prepared in advance to this point. Refrigerate up to 24 hours. To serve, bring to room temperature and bake as directed above.

ZEL'S SQUASH CASSEROLE

2½ pounds summer squash (both yellow and green)
 3 tablespoons dry seasoned bread crumbs
 3 eggs, beaten
 1 tablespoon minced onion
 1 tablespoon butter
   Salt and pepper to taste
 ¼ cup grated sharp Cheddar cheese

Scrub squash and parboil about 15 minutes. Mash squash and drain thoroughly.

In a 2-quart casserole, combine squash, bread crumbs, eggs, onion, butter and salt and pepper. Top with grated cheese.(*) Bake, uncovered, at 350° for 20 to 30 minutes.

Serves 6.

(*)May be prepared in advance to this point. Refrigerate up to 24 hours. To serve, bring to room temperature and bake as directed above.

ZUCCHINI VINAIGRETTE

1½ pounds zucchini
 2 large seedless oranges, peeled and sliced
 1 large red onion, sliced into rings
 ¼ cup olive oil
 3 tablespoons white vinegar
 ¼ teaspoon sugar
 ¾ teaspoon ground coriander
   Salt and pepper to taste

Scrub zucchini and cut into ½-inch circles. Steam until crisp-tender for 5 minutes; cool. Combine zucchini, orange slices and onion in a bowl.

To prepare dressing, combine remaining ingredients in a jar and shake to blend. Toss zucchini mixture with dressing.(*)

Serves 8.

(*)May be refrigerated up to 24 hours.

ZUCCHINI PICKLES

2 pounds zucchini
2 teaspoons mustard seeds
8 fresh dill heads
4 cups water
2 cups white or cider vinegar
2 tablespoons salt

Scrub zucchini and cut into sticks. Divide zucchini between two 1-quart jars. Put half the mustard seeds and half the dill in each jar.

Combine water, vinegar and salt and bring to a boil. Pour over zucchini strips; cover. Refrigerate up to 2 weeks.

2 quarts.

GEORGINA'S ZUCCHINI

5 pounds zucchini
¼ to ½ cup cooking oil
1 cup chopped fresh parsley
1 cup chopped fresh basil
2 cloves garlic, crushed
  Salt and pepper to taste

Scrub zucchini, trim ends and cut into julienne strips. In a large skillet, heat a little of the oil and sauté zucchini with remaining ingredients, adding oil as necessary, until crisp-tender.

Serves 8.

DEEDEE'S ZUCCHINI

2 pounds zucchini, diced
¼ cup butter
½ pound fresh mushrooms, sliced
1 can (8 ounces) water chestnuts, drained and sliced
  Salt and pepper to taste
½ cup grated Gruyère and Monterey Jack cheeses, combined

Steam zucchini 5 minutes. In a large skillet, melt butter and sauté mushrooms until tender.

In a 2-quart casserole, combine zucchini, mushrooms, water chestnuts, salt and pepper. Top with grated cheese mixture.(*) Bake, uncovered, at 350° for 25 to 30 minutes.

Serves 6.

(*)May be prepared in advance to this point. Refrigerate up to 24 hours. To serve, bring to room temperature and bake as directed above.

ZUCCHINI BAKE

1¼ pounds zucchini
4 eggs
¼ cup flour
½ cup grated Parmesan cheese
3 tablespoons sliced green onions
3 tablespoons chopped parsley
1 clove garlic, crushed
¾ teaspoon oregano
1¼ teaspoons salt
¼ teaspoon pepper
18 cherry tomatoes, halved

Scrub zucchini and shred or chop fine (you will have about 4 cups). Press out moisture between paper towels. Combine eggs, flour, ¼ cup of the cheese, the onions, parsley, garlic, oregano, salt and pepper. Stir in zucchini and pour mixture into a greased 1½-quart casserole. Arrange tomato halves, cut side up, on top. Sprinkle with remaining cheese.(*) Bake at 350° for about 30 minutes.

Serves 6.

(*)May be prepared in advance to this point. Refrigerate up to 24 hours. To serve, bring to room temperature and bake as directed above.

ITALIAN-STYLE ZUCCHINI

1 large zucchini
1 cup flour
1 teaspoon salt
¼ teaspoon pepper
2 eggs, beaten
3 tablespoons grated Parmesan cheese
2 tablespoons vegetable oil
2 tablespoons olive oil
1 teaspoon lemon juice
½ teaspoon sugar

Scrub zucchini and slice into thin circles. In a bag, shake zucchini with flour, salt and pepper. Dip floured circles in beaten eggs and then in grated cheese.

In a skillet, combine oils and heat. Fry zucchini over medium heat until golden brown. Spread cooked circles on a platter and sprinkle with lemon juice and sugar. Serve immediately.

Serves 4.

ZUCCHINI-POTATO PANCAKES

4 boiling potatoes
2 medium zucchini
2 eggs, lightly beaten
1½ tablespoons flour
¼ teaspoon baking powder
1 teaspoon salt
Pepper to taste
2 tablespoons grated onion
½ cup vegetable oil

Wash and peel potatoes; grate coarsely and drop in cold water. Trim zucchini and grate coarsely. Drain the potatoes thoroughly and squeeze dry between towels. Combine zucchini and potatoes with eggs, flour, baking powder, salt and pepper. Stir in onion.

Heat oil in a skillet and drop in large spoonfuls of potato-zucchini mixture. Fry on each side until golden brown.(*)

Serves 6 to 8.

(*)May be prepared in advance. Refrigerate up to 24 hours or freeze. Place pancakes between sheets of aluminum foil to keep them from getting soggy. To serve, bring to room temperature and reheat at 450° until crisp, about 10 minutes.

ZUCCHINI CRESCENT PIE

1 can (8 ounces) refrigerator crescent rolls
¾ cup cashews
3 medium zucchini
3 tablespoons butter
½ clove garlic, crushed
¼ teaspoon salt
¼ teaspoon dill weed
⅛ teaspoon pepper
2 eggs, beaten
1 cup cubed Monterey Jack cheese
2 teaspoons chopped parsley

Separate crescent rolls into 8 triangles and press them together in a 10-inch pie plate to form a crust. Sprinkle cashews over crust.

Scrub zucchini and slice into ⅛-inch-thick circles. In a large skillet, melt butter and sauté zucchini until light brown. Add garlic and seasonings and spoon zucchini onto crust. Pour eggs over zucchini, top with cheese and sprinkle with parsley. Bake at 325° for 45 to 50 minutes or until edges are golden brown.(*)

Serves 8 as a main dish.

(*)May be refrigerated up to 24 hours. To serve, bring to room temperature and reheat.

ZUCCHINI BREAD

- 2 cups sugar
- 3 cups flour
- 1 teaspoon baking soda
- ¼ teaspoon baking powder
- 1 teaspoon salt
- 1 teaspoon cinnamon
- 1 cup oil
- 1 teaspoon vanilla
- 3 eggs, beaten
- 2 cups grated raw zucchini, drained
- ½ cup chopped walnuts

Grease 2 loaf pans, 9 x 5 x 3 inches. Place all dry ingredients in a bowl. Make a well in center and add oil, vanilla and eggs; mix well. Add zucchini and nuts. Pour into loaf pans and bake at 325° for 55 minutes. Cool before removing from pans.(*)

2 loaves.

(*)May be refrigerated up to 24 hours or frozen. To serve, bring to room temperature.

PINEAPPLE SQUASH

- 3 small acorn squash (about 2½ pounds)
- ⅓ cup soft butter
  Salt
- 1½ cups drained crushed pineapple
- 1 apple, cored and diced
- 2 tablespoons brown sugar

Scrub squash, cut in half horizontally and scoop out seeds. Steam squash, covered, in a small amount of water 30 minutes; drain. Spread cavities with butter and sprinkle with salt. Combine remaining ingredients and spoon mixture into cavities.(*) Place squash in a 13 x 9 x 2-inch baking dish and bake at 350° for 30 minutes.

Serves 6.

(*)May be prepared in advance to this point. Refrigerate up to 24 hours. To serve, bring to room temperature and bake as directed above.

BUTTERNUT SQUASH CASSEROLE

- 1 butternut squash (about 3 pounds)
- 3 tablespoons butter
- 1 teaspoon salt
- ½ teaspoon cinnamon
- ¼ teaspoon nutmeg
- 2 tablespoons brown sugar

Wash squash and cut in half horizontally. Place both halves, cut side down, in a baking pan and bake at 400° until tender, about 1 hour.

Remove skin and scoop out seeds. Mash squash and mix with remaining ingredients. Turn into a 1-quart casserole.(*) Reduce heat to 350° and bake, uncovered, about 20 minutes to heat through.

Serves 6.

(*)May be prepared in advance to this point. Refrigerate up to 24 hours or freeze. To serve, bring to room temperature and bake as directed above.

WINTER SQUASH SOUFFLE

- ½ cup sugar
- 1 package (10 ounces) frozen winter squash, thawed
- ½ cup flour
- 3 eggs, separated
- ½ teaspoon salt
  Dash each cinnamon and nutmeg
- 2 cups milk
- ¼ cup butter, melted

Add sugar to thawed squash and blend in flour. Beat egg yolks, salt, spices, milk and butter; combine with squash mixture. Beat egg whites until stiff and fold into squash mixture. Spoon into a greased 2-quart soufflé dish (*) and bake at 350° for 50 to 60 minutes.

Serves 4.

(*)May be prepared in advance to this point. Refrigerate up to 24 hours. To serve, bring to room temperature and bake as directed above.

GUACAMOLE TOMATOES

  6 small tomatoes
  1 ripe avocado, peeled, pitted and mashed
  ½ teaspoon chili powder
  1 tablespoon grated onion
  1 tablespoon lemon juice
  ½ teaspoon salt
     Dash pepper

Wash tomatoes, core and scoop out pulp. Chop pulp fine and combine with remaining ingredients. Put mixture into tomato shells and chill at least 4 hours (may be refrigerated up to 24 hours).

Serves 6.

TOMATOES

CHERRY TOMATOES DILLUXE

  1 tablespoon butter
  ½ teaspoon salt
  ¼ teaspoon pepper
  ¼ teaspoon garlic powder
  ½ teaspoon dill weed (¼ teaspoon fresh)
  2 dozen cherry tomatoes

In a large skillet, melt butter and add salt, pepper, garlic powder and dill. Toss in tomatoes to coat them all over with butter sauce. Do not leave in skillet more than a few moments or tomato skins will crack — the tomatoes should remain firm.

Serves 4.

MEXICALI TOMATOES

  2 pints small-curd cottage cheese
  1 can (4 ounces) green chiles, seeded
     and chopped
  ¼ cup chopped stuffed olives
  ½ cup thinly sliced green onions
  ½ teaspoon dill weed
     Salt and pepper to taste
  8 medium tomatoes, peeled
     Lettuce leaves

Combine all ingredients except tomatoes and lettuce and chill at least 1 hour. Slice tomatoes, not quite through, into wedges to form petals of a flower. Arrange on lettuce leaves. Mound cottage cheese mixture into centers of opened tomatoes.(*)

Serves 8.

(*)May be refrigerated up to 48 hours.

TOMATO TARTE

1½ cups flour
½ teaspoon salt
½ cup vegetable oil
3 tablespoons cold water
4 tomatoes, peeled and sliced
  Salt and pepper to taste
2 cups grated Swiss cheese
2 tablespoons flour
4 eggs
2 cups light cream
½ teaspoon salt
  Dash cayenne pepper

Mix 1½ cups flour, ½ teaspoon salt and the oil, blending thoroughly. Sprinkle water on dough, mix well and form into a ball. Roll out to fill a 10-inch pie plate.

Arrange tomatoes on pastry. Sprinkle with salt and pepper. Toss cheese with 2 tablespoons flour and sprinkle over tomatoes. Beat eggs with cream, ½ teaspoon salt and the cayenne; pour over tomatoes.(*) Bake at 375° for 40 minutes or until set. Let cool slightly before serving.

Serves 8.

(*)May be prepared in advance to this point. Refrigerate up to 24 hours or freeze. To serve, bring to room temperature and bake as directed above.

TOMATOES FLORENTINE

1 package (10 ounces) frozen chopped spinach
4 tomatoes
1 tablespoon butter
1 tablespoon flour
½ teaspoon salt
½ cup milk
1 egg, lightly beaten
2 teaspoons butter

Cook spinach according to package directions and drain well. Cut ¼-inch slice off top of each tomato and scoop out pulp, leaving a ¼-inch-thick shell.

To prepare sauce, melt 1 tablespoon butter and stir in flour and salt. Gradually add milk and stir in egg. Add cooked spinach to this sauce. Fill tomatoes with spinach mixture. Top tomatoes with a dot of remaining butter. Place in an 8 x 8 x 2-inch baking dish.(*) Bake at 375° for 20 minutes.

Serves 4.

(*)May be prepared in advance to this point. Refrigerate up to 24 hours. To serve, bring to room temperature and bake as directed above.

TOMATO PUDDING

3 cups fresh white bread cubes
1 can (14 ounces) tomato puree
½ teaspoon salt
¼ cup light brown sugar
2 tablespoons butter
½ cup boiling water

Place bread in a greased 1½-quart casserole. In a saucepan, combine tomato puree, salt, brown sugar, butter and water; bring to a boil. Pour tomato mixture over bread. Cover tightly and bake at 375° for 30 minutes.

Serves 6.

TOMATO SAUCE

3 tablespoon olive oil
1 large Bermuda onion, chopped
½ green pepper, chopped
2 stalks celery, with leaves, chopped
1 carrot, chopped
1 clove garlic, chopped
6 large tomatoes, skinned
½ bay leaf
1 teaspoon light brown sugar
1 teaspoon basil
1 teaspoon salt
⅛ teaspoon pepper

In a large skillet, heat oil and sauté onion, green pepper, celery, carrot and garlic 3 minutes. Add remaining ingredients, cover and cook over moderate heat until thickened, about 45 minutes. Remove bay leaf and blend sauce in a blender or food processor. Correct seasonings if necessary.(*)

To convert this recipe to an Italian-style meat sauce, brown 1 pound ground beef and add to prepared Tomato Sauce with 1 teaspoon oregano. Simmer for 1 hour.

About 4 cups.

(*)May be prepared in advance to this point. Refrigerate up to 72 hours or freeze. To serve, reheat.

A splendid idea for freezing small portions of sauce for individual servings is to pour sauce into paper cups and freeze. Transfer the frozen cups to a plastic bag.

TURNIPS

TURNIP CASSEROLE

2 yellow turnips, peeled and cubed
2 potatoes, peeled and cubed
1 cup sliced green onions
½ cup chicken broth
2 tablespoons butter
½ teaspoon salt

Mix turnips, potatoes and green onions in a greased 2-quart casserole. Pour chicken broth over all, dot with butter and sprinkle with salt.(*) Cover and bake at 350° for 1 hour and 15 minutes, basting occasionally.

Serves 4 to 6.

(*)May be prepared in advance to this point. Refrigerate up to 24 hours. To serve, bring to room temperature and bake as directed above.

WATERCRESS

WATERCRESS CANAPES

¼ cup chopped watercress
1 carton (4 ounces) whipped cream cheese
1 tablespoon mayonnaise
¼ teaspoon salt
¼ teaspoon paprika
12 slices soft white bread
    Soft butter
24 sprigs watercress

Combine chopped watercress, cream cheese, mayonnaise, salt and paprika; reserve.

Remove crusts from bread and roll out each slice very thin. Cut each slice in half. Spread with butter and then with reserved watercress mixture. Arrange a sprig of watercress on each bread slice and roll up like a jelly roll with just a bit of watercress leaves sticking out of one end.(*)

24 canapés.

(*)May be refrigerated up to 24 hours. Cover with waxed paper and top with a damp towel.

VEGETABLE CONCOCTIONS

CURRIED CHEESE HEDGEHOG

2 packages (3 ounces each) cream cheese, softened
6 tablespoons sour cream
2 tablespoons curry powder
1 cup finely chopped pecans
    Chopped parsley

Combine all ingredients except parsley and form into a ball; chill (may be refrigerated up to 48 hours).

When ready to serve, roll ball in chopped parsley and stick all over with raw vegetable spears such as celery, carrots and zucchini. This mixture is also delicious as a stuffing for celery.

About 2 cups.

SWISS VEGETABLE SOUP

1 tablespoon butter
1 clove garlic, minced
1 cup chopped onions
5 chicken bouillon cubes
5 cups hot water
3 medium potatoes, peeled and cut into wedges
3 carrots, scraped and sliced
1 zucchini, sliced
2 stalks celery, chopped, tops reserved
1 tablespoon snipped fresh dill
2 or 3 sprigs parsley, chopped
1 teaspoon salt
½ teaspoon pepper
1 tablespoon cornstarch mixed with
    3 tablespoons cold water

Melt butter and sauté garlic and onions until onions are transparent.

In a large saucepan, dissolve bouillon cubes in hot water. Add all vegetables except the celery tops; then add seasonings. Bring to a boil; reduce heat, cover and simmer 15 to 20 minutes. Add reserved celery tops and continue simmering 10 minutes longer. Stir in cornstarch paste. Cook 2 to 3 minutes longer.(*)

Serves 6.

(*)May be refrigerated up to 72 hours or frozen. When frozen, potatoes tend to get mushy; therefore, add freshly cooked potato wedges when reheating.

LIME VEGETABLE MOLD

    1   package (6 ounces) lime gelatin
    2   cups boiling water
    1   cup cold water
    2   tablespoons vinegar
    ⅓   cup Green Goddess Mayonnaise (below)
    1   cup chopped fresh spinach
    1   cup thinly sliced raw cauliflower
    ¼   cup thinly sliced radishes
    ¼   cup thinly sliced green onions
        Salad greens

Mix gelatin with boiling water to dissolve; add cold water and vinegar. Chill until slightly thickened. Gently stir in remaining ingredients except greens and turn into a greased 2-quart mold. Chill until firm (may be refrigerated up to 48 hours). Unmold and serve on greens.

Serves 8.

Green Goddess Mayonnaise

    1   egg
 1½   tablespoons white wine vinegar
 1½   tablespoons lemon juice
    1   can (2 ounces) anchovy fillets with capers
    1   green onion, chopped
    1   teaspoon tarragon
    1   teaspoon dry mustard
    ¼   teaspoon salt
    ¾   cup chopped parsley
    1   cup vegetable oil
    ½   cup sour cream

Place egg, vinegar, lemon juice, anchovies, onion, tarragon, dry mustard, salt and parsley in a blender or food processor; blend until smooth. Remove cover and, with motor still running, gradually blend in oil. Stir in sour cream and chill (may be refrigerated up to 72 hours).

2 cups.

CRUNCHY SALAD

 1¼   cups thinly sliced radishes
 2¼   cups thinly sliced celery
    ¼   pound fresh mushrooms, sliced
    1   green onion, thinly sliced
    1   jar (6 ounces) marinated artichoke hearts
    ¼   cup olive oil
    2   tablespoons white wine vinegar
    ½   teaspoon sugar
    ½   teaspoon salt
    ¼   teaspoon basil
    ¼   teaspoon oregano
    1   clove garlic, crushed

Combine radishes, celery, mushrooms and green onion; cover and chill. One hour before serving, add artichoke hearts with marinade.

To prepare dressing, combine remaining ingredients in a jar and shake well; chill (may be refrigerated up to 24 hours). When ready to serve, pour dressing over vegetables.

Serves 6.

COUNTRY CASSEROLE

    3   tablespoons vegetable oil
    1   package (10 ounces) frozen chopped spinach, thawed
    2   tablespoons water
    1   medium zucchini, diced
    ½   pound fresh green beans, cut into 1-inch pieces
    1   large onion, chopped
    1   clove garlic, minced
    1   teaspoon fresh basil
    ¾   teaspoon salt
    ⅛   teaspoon pepper
    ¼   teaspoon nutmeg
    4   eggs, slightly beaten
    2   tablespoons grated Parmesan cheese
        Paprika

In a large skillet, heat 2 tablespoons of the oil and cook spinach 2 to 3 minutes. Add remaining oil, the water, zucchini, beans and onion. Cover and cook 10 minutes, stirring occasionally. Add garlic, basil, salt, pepper and nutmeg. Mix well and place in a 1½-quart casserole. Pour beaten eggs over vegetables and sprinkle with cheese.(*) Bake, uncovered, at 350° for 30 minutes. Sprinkle with paprika.

Serves 6.

(*)May be prepared in advance to this point. Refrigerate up to 24 hours. To serve, bring to room temperature and bake as directed above.

HELEN'S
VEGETABLE MEDLEY

- 1 small yellow summer squash, thinly sliced
- 1 small zucchini, thinly sliced
- ½ head cauliflower, broken into flowerets
- ½ Bermuda onion, thinly sliced
- 2 medium tomatoes, quartered
- 1 cup thinly sliced carrots
- 1 cup fresh green beans, cut diagonally into ½-inch slices
- 1 cup diced potatoes
- ½ cup celery, cut diagonally into ½-inch slices
- ¼ cup julienne strips sweet red pepper
- ¼ cup julienne strips green pepper
- ½ cup peas (thawed, if frozen)
- 1 cup beef bouillon
- ⅓ cup olive oil
- 3 cloves garlic, crushed
- 2 teaspoons salt
- 1 small bay leaf, crumbled
- ½ teaspoon savory
- ¼ teaspoon tarragon

Combine vegetables in a 13 x 9 x 2-inch baking dish — do not layer. Bring remaining ingredients to a boil and pour over vegetables. Cover tightly with foil.(*) Bake at 350° for 1 hour and 15 minutes. Stir once or twice.

Serves 8.

(*)May be prepared in advance to this point. Refrigerate up to 24 hours. To serve, bring to room temperature and bake as directed above.

FRESH
VEGETABLE MIX

- 2 tablespoons oil
- 3 potatoes, peeled and thinly sliced
- 1 onion, sliced
- 2 cloves garlic, crushed
- ½ cup water
- 1 medium eggplant, peeled and cubed
- 1 green pepper, cut into ¼-inch strips
- ½ teaspoon thyme
- 1 teaspoon salt
- 1 tablespoon soy sauce
- 2 tomatoes, chopped

In a large skillet, heat oil and sauté potatoes, onion and garlic. Add water, cover and simmer 10 minutes. Mix in eggplant, pepper, thyme and salt. Add more water, if necessary. Cover and cook 10 minutes longer, until vegetables are crisp-tender. Add soy sauce and tomatoes and cook just a minute longer.

Serves 6.

ELYSE'S
VEGETABLE CASSEROLE

- 2 packages (10 ounces each) frozen cut green beans
- 5 tablespoons butter
- 1 pound fresh mushrooms
- 1 can (15 ounces) artichoke hearts, drained
- 2 tablespoons flour
- ½ pint sour cream
- 1 tablespoon grated onion
  Dash sugar
  Salt and pepper to taste
- 2 cups grated Swiss cheese
  Crushed cornflakes

Cook green beans according to package directions; reserve. In skillet, melt 1 tablespoon of the butter and sauté whole mushrooms and artichoke hearts; reserve.

To prepare sauce, melt 2 tablespoons of the butter and stir in flour and sour cream. Add onion, sugar and salt and pepper. In a greased 13 x 9 x 2-inch baking pan, mix sauce and reserved vegetables. Sprinkle with cheese, cover with crushed cornflakes and dot with remaining butter.(*) Bake at 350° for 30 minutes.

Serves 8.

(*)May be prepared in advance to this point. Refrigerate up to 48 hours. To serve, bring to room temperature and bake as directed above.

RATATOUILLE

- 2 tablespoons olive oil
- ½ pound onions, thinly sliced
- 1 pound fresh tomatoes, skinned
- 1 can (16 ounces) tomato puree
- 3 cloves garlic, crushed
  Bouquet garni (parsley, bay leaf, thyme)
- 1 jar (10 ounces) pimiento
- 1 small eggplant, diced
- 2¼ pounds zucchini, diced
  Salt and pepper to taste

In a large skillet, heat oil and brown onions. Add tomatoes, cover and simmer 30 minutes. Mix in tomato puree, garlic, bouquet garni and pimiento. Cover and cook 30 minutes longer. Add diced vegetables and salt and pepper. Cover and simmer 2 hours.(*) May be served hot or cold.

Serves 4 as a main dish.

(*)May be refrigerated up to 72 hours or frozen. To serve, reheat or serve cold.

INDEX

A B C D E